"In SACRED REST, Dr. Dalton-Smith takes readers on a restorative journey. It's a roadmap to healing that you never knew you needed…and a pathway to the serenity you've been longing for."

—Marsha DuCille, editorial director, *CALLED Magazine*

"The fusion of eternal truth and the latest research yields a book that will reset your understanding of what it really means to rest. Dr. Saundra communicates with depth and clarity to challenge and encourage readers to find sacred rest."

—Jennifer Kennedy Dean, executive director of the
Praying Life Foundation; author of *Live a Praying Life*®
and numerous books and Bible studies

"I couldn't be more proud of Dr. Dalton-Smith, a member of my Guild. But even more impressive than Saundra's writing accomplishment is the content of SACRED REST. Everybody I know seems to be busier than ever, sleep-deprived, and in desperate need of rest. I'm guilty too. But Saundra takes a unique approach to the problem, offering eye-opening areas of our lives that need as much rest as our bodies and minds. I learned a ton from it, and you will too."

—Jerry Jenkins, *New York Times* bestselling novelist, biographer,
and owner of the Jerry Jenkins Writers Guild

"Dr. Dalton-Smith has redefined the word *REST*! In a world with constant 'Cerebral Background Noise' you need this book to learn how to set up rest boundaries for you and your family. I love her assessments for the reader to see where there might be a need for more rest, not just in sleep but in the area of mental, spiritual, and CREATIVE rest! I learned so much in this book, I look forward to sharing it with ALL my patients."

—Dr. Angie Welikala, CEO, founder of Healing Agents
International. HealingAgents.org

"As a board-certified clinical neuropsychologist, not a day goes by that I don't have to address the importance of rest with my patients struggling from medical and mental health disorders ranging from attention deficit hyperactivity disorder to post-concussion syndrome. As a society that is now driven by better and faster technology, rest has become a lost art, but no less fundamentally important to our physical, emotional, cognitive, and spiritual well-being. God granted us both time and the model of rest for our good, yet we've come to treat it as a weakness or a punishment. Dr. Dalton-Smith empathizes with the reader's struggle to maintain a lifestyle that includes rest, educates regarding the different types of rest deficit, and passionately shares the gifts and benefits of rest. She weaves her own story and the struggles of others throughout SACRED REST so the reader can relate with the real-life challenge to balance doing with being. SACRED REST should be a mainstay in every clinician's library, and a gift for every friend you care about."

—Dr. Michelle L. Bengtson, board-certified clinical neuropsychologist
and author of *Hope Prevails: Insights From a Doctor's
Personal Journey Through Depression*

"Dr. Saundra Dalton-Smith exhibits the rare combination of physician-inspired medical insights with her faith-driven love for people, which she uses to impart life-enhancing principles and suggestions for living intentionally. Dr. Saundra's passion for seeing women at peace from the inside out is contagious, and Christ followers will discover fresh insights into transforming themselves from mere survivors into women who thrive. Women, whether young or middle-aged or in their senior years will find lots of encouragement and sustenance for their souls."

—Michele Howe, author of 19 books for women, including *Empty Nest,
What's Next?* and *Caring for Our Aging Parents*

"I found myself pausing to breathe deeply just reading through the table of contents for SACRED REST. The pages that followed offered the 'why' and 'how' we can slow down. Dr. Saundra helps us to see rest as the gift it is intended to be. I will find myself coming back to her words again and again."

—Esther Fleece, speaker and author of *No More Faking Fine*

SACRED
REST

SACRED REST

RECOVER YOUR LIFE,
RENEW YOUR ENERGY,
RESTORE YOUR SANITY

SAUNDRA
DALTON-SMITH, MD

New York Nashville

Copyright © 2017 by Saundra Dalton-Smith

Cover design by Edward A. Crawford
Cover photography by Getty Images
Cover copyright © 2017 by Hachette Book Group, Inc.

FaithWords
Hachette Book Group
1290 Avenue of the Americas, New York, NY 10104
faithwords.com
twitter.com/faithwords

First Edition: December 2017

FaithWords is a division of Hachette Book Group, Inc. The FaithWords name and logo are trademarks of Hachette Book Group, Inc.

The publisher is not responsible for websites (or their content) that are not owned by the publisher.

The Hachette Speakers Bureau provides a wide range of authors for speaking events. To find out more, go to www.hachettespeakersbureau.com or call (866) 376-6591.

Library of Congress Cataloging-in-Publication Data
Names: Dalton-Smith, Saundra.
Title: Sacred rest : recover your life, renew your energy, restore your sanity / Dr. Saundra Dalton-Smith.
Description: First edition. | New York : Faith Words, [2017] | Includes bibliographical references.
Identifiers: LCCN 2017029725| ISBN 9781478921677 (hardcover) | ISBN 9781478923589 (audio download) | ISBN 9781478921660 (ebook)
Subjects: LCSH: Rest—Religious aspects—Christianity.
Classification: LCC BV4597.55 .D35 2017 | DDC 248.4/6—dc23
LC record available at https://lccn.loc.gov/2017029725

ISBN: 978-1-4789-2167-7 (hardcover), 978-1-4789-2166-0 (ebook)

Printed in the United States of America

LSC-H

10   9   8   7   6

To my sons, Tristan and Isaiah, may you never become so busy you neglect to enjoy the life you create.

Contents

Foreword   *xi*

How to Use This Book   *xiii*

PART I
WHY REST?

1. Living the Burned-Out Life   3
2. The Secret Life of the Well Rested   11
3. The Rest You've Been Missing   23
4. Physical Rest   33
5. Mental Rest   47
6. Emotional Rest   55
7. Spiritual Rest   65
8. Social Rest   77
9. Sensory Rest   87
10. Creative Rest   95
11. Give It a Rest   105
12. Finding a Sweet Place to Land   113

PART II
THE GIFTS OF REST

13. The Gift of Boundaries   123
14. The Gift of Reflection   131

15. The Gift of Freedom 139
16. The Gift of Acceptance 147
17. The Gift of Exchange 153
18. The Gift of Permission 159
19. The Gift of Cessation 165
20. The Gift of Art 173
21. The Gift of Communication 179
22. The Gift of Productivity 185
23. The Gift of Choice 191
24. The Gift of Faith 195

PART III
THE PROMISES OF REST

25. I Choose My Best Life 205

Personal Rest Deficit Assessment Tool *211*
Thirty-Day Sacred Rest Challenge *215*
Acknowledgments *217*
Notes *219*
About the Author *225*

Foreword

Is rest elusive or obtainable? Over eight million people in the United States struggle to fall asleep or stay asleep each and every night. According to the National Sleep Foundation, 45 percent of Americans say that poor or insufficient sleep affected their daily activities at least once a week. This epidemic has led to poor job performance, depression, and overall dissatisfaction with quality of life and productivity. *Sacred Rest* by Dr. Saundra Dalton-Smith offers hope and answers through proven solutions found in spiritual renewal.

For some, sleep deprivation is only a brief problem. But finding genuine "rest" is more than overcoming insomnia. *Sacred Rest* discusses, wrestles with, and answers the "how" question and more. Rest for the body, mind, and spirit may appear to be hard to find because hurry is outside of us and inside of us. Daily we are left to wonder, *Is rest possible?*

Sacred Rest is born from a place of personal experience. Dr. Dalton-Smith, an internal medicine physician, practices full-time and is also a wife and mother of two elementary-age boys. The author slipping off the edge of burnout, risks sharing her own story, becoming raw and real in the process. It's in this place of vulnerability and personal growth that she invites the reader to share her journey.

This essential book is divided into three parts: "Why Rest?" discussing the practical aspects of rest; "The Gifts of Rest," discussing the spiritual aspects of rest; and "The Promises of Rest," in which the author presents the reader a challenge to go deeper into rest. There are biblical solutions backed with thorough medical research and practical applications throughout.

Rest is obtainable, Dr. Dalton-Smith reminds us. "Inertia is a healing place, where stillness leads to recovery of the body's natural ability to heal itself. Sleeping and napping are the two most common types of passive rest. Sleep is not an option. Whether or not you choose to lay your body down, eventually your body will shut down. Sleep is required for health. It is not the foundation of rest, but the by-product of rest."

Are you weak, weary, or worn out? What are you waiting for? *Sacred Rest* is entirely available and obtainable. The choice is yours. Join the community and commit the next 30 days to seek and find *Sacred Rest*. I will see you there.

—Dr. Sheryl Giesbrecht, author of *Get Back Up: Trusting God When Life Knocks You Down*, speaker, radio and television personality, global influencer. www.FromAshesToBeauty.com www.HSBN.tv

How to Use This Book

Welcome, Friend,

I want to take a few minutes before you begin to give you a quick peek at what you will find inside this book. Think of *Sacred Rest* as a lavish buffet, not a Happy Meal. It has been purposely written in short chapters to make it easy to fit into your busy schedule, but don't rush through it. Rushing has overwhelmed us with the things of life, and in the process, we miss opportunities to enjoy life. My desire in writing this book is to see you cherishing each bite of the good things daily placed before you.

Think of me as your Sunday school–teaching girlfriend who just happens to be board certified in internal medicine. If we were chatting over coffee, one minute I might share with you a great article I read in a medical journal and the next I'm raving over the sticky pastry we just devoured as we open our Bibles to study Ephesians together. That's real life. It's messy and complicated yet filled with moments of goodness, togetherness, and truth. I've found rest to be the compass directing me to all three and much more.

In part I, "Why Rest?," I discuss the practical aspects of rest. Each chapter in this section will help you understand different types of rest through the use of stories, research, reflection, and application. In part II, "The Gifts of Rest," I discuss the spiritual aspects of rest. These chapters have biblical insight on how rest, or the lack thereof, affects every area of your life. In part III, "The Promises of Rest," I end our time together with a challenge to go deeper into rest and witness its effect in your life.

I don't know where you stand physically, emotionally, or spiritually today. If you are most in need of encouragement, before you dive into the practical application of rest, I welcome you to begin with part II. Yes, you heard me right. You get to choose. *Sacred Rest* isn't a generic four-step system to guarantee sweet sleep and even sweeter days. The process to recover your life, renew your energy, and regain your sanity is uniquely different for every person. Enjoy the journey as you unwrap what rest means for you.

—*Dr. Saundra*

PART I

WHY REST?

"When I am resting because my body is weak, I need to remember that I'm not wasting the day doing nothing. I am doing exactly what I need to do. I'm recovering."

AUTHOR UNKNOWN

Chapter 1

Living the
Burned-Out Life

There should be a "Get Out of Your Responsibilities" card you can play on those days when life is just too difficult, days when everything within you wants a moment simply to be still. That thought flittered through my mind as I lay stretched out on the foyer floor.

The weight of an unexamined life lies heavy against the heart of the weary. Pushing and pushing until it nudges you right past sanity into the pits. Thankfully, lying supine on a hardwood floor can be therapeutic for the soul.

I never knew how hauntingly healing cold wooden planks could be for the body. I never realized the many facets of peace and rest available when you lay yourself down on purpose. Peace comes in many forms. On this day it came in a ten-minute reprieve in the middle of the chaos that had become my life. There was no time to break away and do it right. No time for any long, drawn-out me-time ritualistic activities. No mani-pedi. No hot tea and biscuits. No caramel macchiato. No Dead Sea salt–infused bath.

No, on this day, time would not allow me to bury my exhaustion in any of my normal vices. So, I did what any sane burned-out human would do after picking up the kids from day care. I set them in front of the TV with a snack, and I lay on the floor. I stretched out my back against the boards, palms down, and closed my eyes. In that moment of focused ceasing, I felt the beginning of peace stir within my body.

Peace came slowly. It was as if God himself breathed a divine exhalation, releasing new strength into me. I inhaled it. I clung to the moment, needing it to last just a little longer. I needed even more to satisfy my *longing* for rest. Not a desire for more sleep, but a yearning to be soul-free. Come to think of it, maybe it wasn't that I needed to be filled, but rather, I needed to pour out. Regardless of which direction the energy was flowing, something powerful was happening on that floor.

The voices of my children rang out with laughter as they delighted over the antics of the cartoon they watched. Inwardly I laughed along with them. The smile creeping on my lips was only mildly disturbed by the dog licking my face and the toddler crawling over my leg. It was sloppy peace, but it was mine. It was peace in the middle of a mental storm.

I could complain, but it would be futile. If I'm completely honest, I'm to blame for this storm. I created it. I fueled it. I continually recruit and pull others into it with me. I didn't mean to do it. It is just a reality of the life I created.

You see, I'm a doer. If I'm not doing something, I'm wasting my time. At least that is what I thought, until a few years ago when I found myself looking up from a compromising position into the face of my smug husband asking, "What in the world are you doing on the floor?"

Only one answer came to mind—*burning*. A single thought that, at the time, seemed so misplaced and irrelevant I almost didn't say it out loud. At times I wish I hadn't.

His smirk faltered when the first tear fell. I came undone. He kneeled by my side when the floodgates broke. Me. The strong one. The one with the to-do list for her to-do list. The organizer. The planner. When my husband asked what I was doing there on the floor, the image that came to mind was that of kindling being consumed by fire. I was the kindling.

I was burned out, and the life I had created was consuming all I held valuable. But on this day, I was kindling being consumed by an eternal fire. A fire with the power to destroy the heaviness of busyness and ignite a hunger to tap into the source of this strange, sloppy rest I found. Hunger to draw nearer to the sacred sanctuary of rest. I desperately needed to find that place.

Let's be honest; we are all just too busy. I'm too busy to write this book, and you are probably too busy to read this book. Both of us are being pulled by our busy lives when all we want is to have a good life. And so we find ourselves in the inevitable predicament of much activity and little enjoyment. Our wheels spin as we shove more to do in a day with no available daylight hours left, only to find ourselves wanting in the end. Not wanting more to do. No, we have plenty to do. We find ourselves wanting more time to do the things we enjoy doing.

We want time to enjoy our kids. We want time to make love to our spouses. We want time to linger over a good meal. We want time to use the bathroom without interruptions. We want more time.

But there is no more time. Time is. It is both infinite and finite. It goes on and on. With or without us it will continue. Our number of days are known by God alone. Time chimes in loudly over the roar of our anxious minds, initiating a battle between warring fears and courageous rest.

Aborting rest empties me of everything holy. It strips me of the ability to treasure life and peels away the value of being. I feel I'm nothing if I'm doing nothing. My worth is wrapped tight around my endless activity. So I keep going round and round, each time becoming more short-tempered, more disgruntled, and more discontented.

A life without periods of rest will not endure the daily grind.

Rest is not for weaklings. Hollowing out space for rest is work. Finding time for rest is the hands and feet of the promises we long to claim. It means saying no. It means having limits with ourselves. It means having limits with others. It takes courage to rest in the midst of an outcome-driven society. It takes strength to walk away from good in the pursuit of better.

The people-pleaser in me would rather say yes and omit the rest. I've found through the years that I can't please anyone including myself when I'm burned out. Funny how everyone can smell the char of your slow burn except the one standing in the fire.

Sleep Is Not Rest

Have you ever tried to fix your chronically tired self by purposely sleeping a few extra hours on the weekend, only to wake up feeling like you've never rested at all? You had great intentions, but missed one vital piece of the puzzle: Sleep is not rest. As different parts of an intricate system, sleep and rest are designed to work together to ensure every part of you has a way to regenerate and be restored.

If I were sitting across from you right now, our conversation might go something like the one I had with a friend many years ago. It was early one morning, and we were preparing to start a long shift as interns at the hospital: "I'm so tired," lamented my red-eyed friend. Her hair was in a messy ponytail, and her scrubs were wrinkled in all the wrong places. It looked like she had rolled out of bed and stumbled into work on accident.

"What time did you turn in last night?" I asked.

"That's the thing!" she exclaimed. "It's pointless! It doesn't matter if I sleep five hours or ten. I always wake up exhausted. I need a double espresso latte. You want anything?"

Twenty minutes later she returned with two steaming cups of java goodness. I'm convinced heaven must smell like hazelnut coffee. We sipped and reenergized as we discussed each patient's case. I don't know what she had the barista put in those cups, but it was more like liquid octane than percolated ground beans. My heart skipped a beat trying to catch the rhythm of this potent brew. We tackled our hospital rounds that day as if our life soundtrack were shouting, "This girl is on fire!"

A few hours later, we crashed hard, and I do mean hard. I'm pretty sure I was drooling on the student-lounge couch when I awoke. I slept but woke even more drained.

"We need more coffee," my friend declared.

I wasn't sure I could handle another round of her coffee, so I opted to chat.

"Why do you think sleep isn't helping our fatigue? I'm more tired now than I was before we fell asleep."

"I wish I knew. When I was in college, I could sleep like a baby. The second my head hit the pillow I'd be out. In medical school, I started having trouble falling asleep. At first, it took five to ten minutes before I could go to sleep. Now it can take up to an hour when I lie down at night."

"Wow, an hour. As tired as you are at the end of a shift, I would have thought you'd fall asleep quickly," I mused.

"I know, right? But that's the thing; good sleep is gentle. It comes in quietly, descends upon you, and replenishes you. Bad sleep comes in like a flood, overtakes you, and leaves you feeling spent. It's the good I'm missing."

Sleep is a biological necessity. Trying to omit it will slow your productivity and eventually kill you. In an attempt to check this life function off our to-do list every night, many of us have settled for sleep at any cost and of any quality. Our problem isn't simply a need for more sleep. Our problem is that we are missing the good.

Sleep is different from rest, but good-quality sleep trickles down from a life well rested. We may sleep in response to rest, but resting doesn't require us to be in a state of sleep. Sometimes as my friend confessed, sleep is not restful at all. Then there are also those times when even with a lack of sleep, we surprisingly feel rested and ready to tackle the day. The deciding factor is the difference between good sleep and bad sleep.

Nightly we attempt to enter into the five stages of sleep, non-REM stages one to four and stage-five REM. High-quality sleep begins in stage three of non-REM sleep when your brain ceases active processing. You lose your conscious awareness about your surroundings. Your brain and body both enter a quiet state. Bad sleep is fitful and devoid of calm. The mind may wander sporadically over the events of the day, and you may find your legs restlessly moving in response to the pent-up tension in your muscles.

There has to be a bridge between good and bad sleep, and that bridge is rest. Sleep is solely a physical activity. Rest, however, penetrates into the spiritual. Rest speaks peace into the daily storms your mind, body, and spirit encounter. Rest is what makes sleep sweet.

You may pride yourself on your ability to accomplish much each day, but when your natural strengths are taken to the extreme, they can become a liability. Sadly, many of us spend too much of our days doing and not enough of our days being. We have decided rest is not necessary and replaced it with even more activity. I don't have a problem with productive people. I have a problem with worn-out productive people. These are the majority of the faces that grace my medical office, including homeschooling moms, business executives, shift workers, and young professionals. They present me with a list of symptoms, demanding answers and wanting quick fixes to problems that require slowing down.

It may sound like I'm judging, but be assured I am not. I'm part of the same tribe. I've burned the candle at both ends enough for us both and have seen its destructive effects in my life as well as that of thousands of others.

Can you be 100 percent honest with me? With yourself? How is your maxed-out, stressed-out, multitasking life working for you? Is all your activity getting the results you desire?

Since you picked up this book, I would guess your answer to my last question is a resounding no. Let me share a little medical secret with you. The most underused chemical-free, safe, effective, alternative medicine is spelled R-E-S-T: **R**ecognize your risk, **E**valuate your current position, **S**cience and research, **T**oday's application. I'll explain the R-E-S-T method further in chapter 3.

Chapter 2

The Secret Life
of the Well Rested

*"Sometimes it's important to work for that pot of gold. But other
times it's essential to take time off and make sure your most important decision in the day simply consists of choosing which color to
slide down on the rainbow."*[1]

DOUGLAS PAGELS

Karen was a new patient who came to my office with a list of complaints so long I thought she was a hypochondriac. No human could
have a list of ails that complex. However, she most certainly did, and
she was convinced there was a medical reason for her problems. I
think she would have been thankful if I had diagnosed her with something horrible. Nothing is scarier than the unknown. At least with a
definitive diagnosis, she would know what she was up against. She
was a woman desperate for answers. The lack of understanding had
become debilitating. She needed to know why her body ached and
why she struggled to concentrate. She needed to know it wasn't all in
her head. She was a simmering pot of anxiety with a dash of insomnia

stirred by relentless daily stress. Her discontentment was consuming her, and it seeped into her relationship with her husband and her children. Her life failed to live up to the claims of what marriage, family, and career are supposed to offer. All she had strived to achieve, all that she had fought to have, was betraying her, or so it seemed.

Karen's list of complaints included the following:

- feeling tired and exhausted all the time
- feeling like nothing she did at home or work made a difference or was appreciated
- catching colds and getting sick more than others
- feeling detached from her family and friends
- having a negative outlook on life
- experiencing frequent headaches, neck pain, and muscle soreness
- moving easily to anger and irritation with those she interacted
- growing dependent on food, pills, and wine to help her feel better
- feeling depressed and stressed out

I listened as she rattled off her list, and I gave her the benefit of the doubt. There are many chronic diseases and chronic medical disorders capable of making you tired all the time. Unfortunately, there are just as many people with a chronic rest deficit, and the symptoms can look the same. But unlike many chronic illnesses, a chronic rest deficit can be cured.

The question is, what kind of tired are you?

Fatigue can result from our overindulgent schedules, lack of quality sleep, an unhealthy diet, thyroid and hormone imbalances, adrenal failure, medication side effects, anxiety or depression, or feeling a lack of purpose and lack of motivation. The list of fatigue boosters is endless. Determining the cause is the challenging part of health care.

Nevertheless, I examined Karen and ordered tests to check for the most common causes of fatigue. Every test came back within the proper range and declared all was well medically.

"You are perfectly healthy," I announced.

Karen was furious. Her face flushed hot, and her breathing came in short, frantic bursts. Her eyes pierced through me. My happy declaration of health had wounded her. Her behavior reminded me of a show I'd seen called *When Animals Attack!* I debated yelling for my nurse to bring in a sedative shot. Before I could make up my mind to yell or to run, her rant began.

"Why can't you doctors figure out what's wrong with me?"

She said more than that, much of which I refuse to repeat in a book my kids or parents may choose to read. Sometimes people want to hear the truth, and sometimes they just want to hear what they want to hear. In medicine, it's helpful to determine when someone's ready to confront their inner issues. I'm often contemplating when is the right time to bring up smoking cessation with my chain-smokers or weight loss with my Krispy Kreme lovers. It is even more difficult to confront someone dealing with a lack of rest. No cigarette or donut can satisfy a body hungry for rest. Add a whopping dose of rage to the tiredness, and you've got a person who is in no mood to listen to anything you have to say. The only way to break through is to let the weary diagnose themselves. I needed Karen to start looking at her list in a new way.

"Karen, I think your problem is not solely a medical one. I think you are suffering from a chronic rest deficit. In your list, you named multiple areas of your life under attack by chronic fatigue, chronic hopelessness, and a chronic lack of joy. This is not just a medical issue; it's a mind-body-spirit issue. Your healing has to come from the inside out. Once you restore the needed rest in your life, you will see the changes you desire."

"It can't be a lack of rest!" she protested. "I've tried massages. I've taken vacations. I have even been working with a spiritual counselor. I should be the most restful woman in town."

Karen was aware of how rest affected every area of her life. She had made attempts to improve but to no avail. It was during this same time I too was going through my own personal revelation about how different types of rest affected me. Like Karen, I had attempted all the common recommendations of the self-help gurus. Either we were both too broken for repair or their theory of rest was missing something. The optimist in me refused to accept brokenness as a resting place.

I needed to open Karen's mind to the likelihood of rest, or more accurately her lack of rest, as the underlying cause of her life crisis. Her answers to the following questions helped illuminate the possibility of a rest imbalance. Take a minute to answer these questions for yourself.

- Do you often feel tired when you wake up in the morning?
- Do you find yourself having difficulty concentrating?
- Are your emotions easily affected by the actions of others?
- Do you suffer from headaches, muscle aches, or generalized fatigue with no known medical diagnosis?
- Are your relationships with others strained because of your inability to stay connected?
- Do you find yourself spending more time doing things you *have* to do rather than things you *want* to do?

- Has your view of life lost its <u>expectation</u> of excitement and adventure? *yes*
- *no* • Do you struggle to stay awake and focused when reading or watching TV?
- *yes* • Do you depend on quick energy fixes like caffeine or sugar to help you get through the day?
- *yes* • Do you find yourself craving comfort items at night like ice cream or wine to help you wind down?
- *no* • Are you prone to abrupt moments of anger or unexplainable fits of crying?
- *no* • Do you often feel like your life is out of control?

Karen's answers pointed toward a life in danger of drowning in responsibilities with no lifesaver in sight. She had tried many things to correct and improve her situation, all to no avail. <u>She was aware of her impending burnout but had dismissed her restlessness as a possible cause for her symptoms.</u> Karen had given up on rest and placed it in the same pile as the unread books sitting on the nightstand. Rest was waiting around for her to get to it, and she never did.

<u>My research and observations on rest revealed a gaping hole in our definition of rest.</u> Rest had become synonymous with sleep or a cessation of all activity. But what if <u>rest is in itself a vital activity required to tend to the garden of our lives? What if rest is the water that replenishes the dryness? What if rest is fertilizer awakening us to growth and greatness? What if rest is the hands of the gardener pulling up the weeds threatening to edge out beauty?</u>   ♡

All rest is not created equal. Much of what we consider rest fails to work because it is not restful. Shifting our activities or changing the location of where we are active is no more restful than doing those same activities at home. <u>The most effective rest occurs when we are</u>

purposefully reviving the parts of our life we regularly deplete. Any so-called rest that does not meet this goal isn't rest; it's just more work adding to the busyness.

Rest Solutions That Don't Work

Vacations

Karen's dream vacation sounded like a luxury hospital stay. Her desired activities were to sleep in, eat room service, and enjoy the scenery of a nice room away from home. She planned each family vacation trip with the hope of leaving happier and more rested than when she arrived. Her visions were filled with days of sitting on the beach with the sun warming her body, listening to the ocean serenade her. Unfortunately, her schedule was usually overshadowed by fun activities she knew her kids and her husband would enjoy. Instead of going to bed rested each night, she fell into bed spent from the day's activities. She had a wonderful time on vacation, but vacations were not restful. Vacations were work. She was more exhausted after her vacations than when she left. She needed a vacation to recover from her vacations. In addition to the physical, mental, and emotional exhaustion she already felt before each trip, she now had a week of emails and papers to deal with when she returned to her office.

Vacations are great opportunities to experience new things and explore new places, but they often fail to pour back into our restless lives to the degree needed to resuscitate them. What is the one souvenir every vacationer would love to take home? Time. The gift of being at rest, free from schedules and agendas. Even if Karen succeeded in spending one week focusing on meeting her needs, it would be insufficient to sustain the fifty-one remaining weeks in her year. It would be like giving a starving child one bowl of rice and saying, "Now that you're temporarily satiated you should be good." Consistent goodness is needed to truly satisfy, nourish, and restore.

Downsizing

Downsizing an overwhelming life sounds like a good idea. If there are too many activities, then scaling them down should alleviate the congestion. Karen placed limits on the number of activities her kids could participate in. She limited her involvement with volunteer work and social engagement. She created extra margin in her life and anticipated using that time for the things she loved. Unfortunately, the human default mechanism is to do what's easy rather than what's beneficial. It's easy to flick on the TV and recline on the sofa with a bowl of Ben & Jerry's. It would be heavenly if somewhere between the spoon, our mouth, and a great sitcom story line, we could find everything we need for happiness. But escapism is not rest; there are not enough spoonfuls of Chunky Monkey to propel us toward the life we desire. Downsizing your life without a restful plan for filling the gaps only opens the door for other enemies like laziness and apathy.

Medications

Karen was dependent on sleeping pills. They succeeded in giving her six to eight hours of sleep but failed to leave her feeling rested. She could not fall asleep without taking them. Each night she would go through her routine of lying in the bed attempting to fall asleep, hoping that this night she would not have to take anything. She would toss and turn for hours only to relent to her need for sleep. Other nights her mind would keep her up mulling over thoughts, conversations, and emotions from the day. Medicated sleep was better than no sleep, even if it left her mentally handicapped the next day. The drugs lingered in her system, forcing her to push through a drugged fog the following morning. Sleeping pills are not successful at providing quality rest. Their goal is simply to get you to sleep. Rest will still be required, and it does not respond to medications.

Sleep Marathons

For those capable of sleeping, you may be tempted to participate in weekly sleep marathons. Weekdays are spent staying up late to fit in a great movie you've wanted to see or that drama everyone's talking about at work. You crash hard at night and easily fall asleep, but you struggle to get up each morning. The weekends are your time to play catch-up. You trade your normal six hours for ten hours on Saturday and Sunday. You sleep until your body hurts from having been in bed for so long. You wake up with a sleep hangover. Head pounding and mouth dry, you wonder why you feel so horrible. You got extra sleep, but it left you more depleted than the days you wake up on schedule. These sleep marathons are more harmful than helpful. The prolonged time without food sends your body into a fasting state. Since the body isn't getting the energy it desires, it begins breaking down muscle and fat for energy. It's like being in a marathon with no medal at the end. Sleep marathons are destructive to your health. Rest never destroys.

Multitasking

If you can get more done faster, maybe you can have more time for yourself. That is the lie of multitasking. It assumes your brain can focus efficiently on numerous tasks at one time and do each optimally. Multitasking fatigues your mental resources. It splits your attention between activities and increases the potential for errors, impairs your judgment, and reduces performance. Multitasking does not lead to more time for rest. If you allocate time to complete each task before moving to the next, you will find you finish faster than you would multitasking. Well-rested people do not exponentially multiply their activities; they divide and conquer.

Complaints

Karen spent a lot of energy complaining about how she felt rather than using that energy in a more productive way. She chose to idolize her fatigue and lack of mental clarity rather than do the necessary work to change it. As she sat before me with her list of complaints, I began to wonder if she was unwilling to change or just didn't know what to change.

At one point in the conversation, I'd heard all I cared to hear. I closed my laptop and turned on my stool to face Karen. I could see she was unsure what was happening. She continued to ramble on, looking between me and my computer. I was no longer typing in any of the information she was sharing. Eventually, she stopped talking. I couldn't help smiling at the bewilderment on her face. My mind juggled an idea I quickly dismissed. It was crazy, but sometimes the unusual opens the door to the miraculous. I figured *Why not?* and jumped right in.

"Karen, what you need I can't provide in a fifteen-minute office visit. Since we both have cell phones, I'm willing for the next thirty days to send you a text. All I ask is that you read each text and do what it says daily."

"No. I don't have time for that. I need help! Are you going to help me?" she jabbed.

"Are you going to help yourself?" I countered. "If you can't give yourself the few minutes to do what I'm suggesting, then no one can help you."

In the weeks leading up to Karen's visit, I had been applying my findings on rest to my life. It was the hardest easy work I'd ever done. People-pleasing, workaholic go-getters don't excel at rest without an internal battle. Rest requires submission of the soul, and the soul wants what the soul wants. It fights back against rest by holding up all the pretty fruit busyness is producing. It never gives you time to cut inside that same fruit to see the rot and decay at the core, decay that will inevitably surface when you're ready to take a bite into the busy life you've created.

Slap.

Karen was no longer satisfied possessing a life that looked good on the surface. She wanted a life dripping with sweet nectar and daily opportunities to taste its pleasure. As much as she doubted rest as the answer, she was sick and tired of being sick and tired. She agreed to join me in a Sacred Rest Challenge. For thirty days I would send her a daily rest prompt. What she didn't know was that each prompt focused on restoring a specific type of rest in her life.

Rest is not a one-size-fits-all commodity. In this book, I am not attempting to give you an XYZ approach to an instantly happy life. For one reason, it does not exist. For another, your personal rest prescription is as individualized as your DNA. What I am promising is that as you begin to understand the role rest plays in your life you will do the following:

- replace the stress of intense living with the peace of intentional rest
- identify your rest deficit and discover which types of rest you need most
- recover your life from the effects of a chronic rest deficit
- renew your energy and experience the benefits of a well-rested life
- restore your sanity by claiming the gifts of rest

- exchange the guilt of your unfinished to-do list for the freedom to choose best
- overcome being overwhelmed by the life you've worked so hard to create

A Well-Rested Life

A few months later Karen returned to see me. In her arms, she carried a pink leather-bound journal. The toughness she had displayed in her first visit was now softened by the deep watering of a well-rested life. Her strength was reinforced and made even more lovely in the sacredness of rest.

OCTOBER 15

Light shone through my sheer curtains announcing the dawn. Its presence inviting a transition out of the darkness. I rolled over to look at the alarm clock. For the second week this month, I had awoken minutes before it chimed. Instead of hitting snooze two to three times, today I turned the alarm off. Its shrill plea for me to greet the day was no longer needed. Time has ceased being my enemy. I am amazed. My only regret was not listening to the cry of my heart earlier and surrendering to rest.

OCTOBER 18

It's Saturday, and normally I would be up trying to do all the things I don't have time to do during the week. A pot of dark roast and I'm good for a least 3 hours. Rest is now my drug of choice. It both awakens and relaxes me. Today I spent 20 minutes outside my home walking and praying. Amber and ruby leaves lined my path.

The fall wind blew heavy against my back, pushing me forward. I declared it all good. It quenched my hunger for more and silenced the lie of busy. Years of busy have kept me in a constant state of slumber. I stand awake physically, mentally, spiritually and emotionally. In the still of the morning, I contemplate the day. Expectations without the burden of guilt. I need today more than today needs me.

OCTOBER 23

Gratitude floods me. I see qualities in my kids I've hoped for. Their independence equally frightens and thrills me. They have proven to be capable of doing much more than I had given them credit. I'm laying down responsibilities that were no longer mine to carry. If only I had stepped back to observe their growth sooner, but I won't bemoan the lost time. I'm taking them ice skating after school. Falling and getting back up, that's what we've been doing as a family. Thankful for the bumps and bruises leading us to better balance.

Karen's journal entries reflected the rhythm of rest she was now enjoying. Thankfully she was desperate enough to try something different, and her life was made better for it. She recovered her life from her addiction to busy and found the secret to living well rested. It isn't in the number of hours slept. It isn't in the number of meditations, prayers, or mental exercises completed. It isn't in quitting your job or blowing off obligations. The secret life of the well rested is found in answering one key question.

What type of rest have you been missing?

Chapter 3

The Rest You've Been Missing

"Nothing satisfies like chocolate," declared the screen saver on Cynthia's laptop as she closed it and placed it in her bag. She had found satisfaction to be an interesting concept. It was an enigma, deeply desired yet dauntingly distant. What then satisfies? This life is full of many things. Her life was full of many things. None of it satisfied her the way she had hoped.

She climbed into her beloved BMW pondering these things as she merged onto the interstate for her commute home. Many thoughts came to mind. She contemplated where she was at this current stage in her life. Thirty was not what she had envisioned. She had believed that by now she would be married with kids, but this was not her reality. She had anticipated traveling abroad. Her expired unstamped passport sat stuffed in her nightstand mocking her plans. She knew something had to give. Something had to change. She simply could not see the next steps needed to move forward, but she knew vision had to come quickly, or she was going to fall hard. She wanted to find satisfaction. She needed to find it, and she knew chocolate wasn't the answer. At five foot five and over two hundred pounds, Cynthia knew chocolate intimately, and she knew the screen saver on her laptop lied. Chocolate did not satisfy.

The music blared on her car radio as she headed down the interstate deep in thought. Her mind played through the different possible scenarios of what could be part of her upcoming life changes. Job opportunities, relationships, and trips—there were so many choices. Actually, there were too many, and that was part of the problem.

She was oblivious to the cars moving around her, yet she stayed in sync with the moving river of metal. She never knew what hit her. When the driver in front of her quickly changed lanes to avoid hitting the braking car in front, Cynthia remained lost in thought until the red brake light broke through her daydreaming. The car behind her was too close and failed to slow down. She didn't see change coming. It bumped right into her comfortable life, sending her into a tailspin and knocking her into a ravine. For a few brief moments, time slowed and accelerated at once. Her thoughts all seemed to move even faster than her spinning vehicle. As her car settled into the ditch and she lost her grasp on the present, she drifted into sleep to the sound of Kelly Clarkson singing "What doesn't kill you makes you stronger."

After Cynthia had arrived at the ER, she was assigned to my medical service. Two days after her accident, she awoke to the melodic sound of the mechanical ventilator pushing breath in and out of her lungs and to the reality of the numerous injuries she had sustained. She scanned the ICU suite, taking in the different machines in the room, trying to understand why tubes and contraptions were all over her body. She watched the nurse at her side manipulating her chest tube and winced as a jolt of pain rose from the place touched. She closed her eyes and tried to remember what happened. How had she gotten here? What had occurred that forced her to be in this place, broken, injured, and hurting?

One of her lungs had collapsed on impact, which was likely the reason she blacked out on the scene. EMS had to extract her from her totaled car. Many CT scans and X-rays later, doctors determined she had numerous rib fractures, a pneumothorax from her punctured lung, a broken femur, and a grade 2 liver laceration that threatened to bleed if aggravated. Her mental exam was consistent with a moderate concussion.

I watched her from the ICU door. Fear was evident in her eyes. Fear was a response I expected. Fear always comes with unexpected change. I've found fear to be a pathetic enemy. Hopelessness is what truly kills. In those few moments of observation, I was looking for signs of hopelessness. Cynthia gave me none. She surveyed the room like a lioness preparing for the hunt. She was obviously weary, but her gaze was full of life. Full of plans, full of dreams, full of possibility, full of hope, full of everything needed for restoration and recovery. It was time for formal introductions.

"Hi Cynthia, I'm Dr. Dalton-Smith. I know all this is a little scary, but let me explain. You were in a car accident. You broke a few bones, and one of your lungs collapsed. Yesterday you had surgery to fix your broken leg. You have a concussion and have been asleep for two days. Welcome back. Now it's time to recover your life."

She stared blankly back at me as if she didn't understand what I was saying. Then I noticed her lips trying to move around the endotracheal tube in her mouth. She was unable to verbalize what she wanted to say, so I grabbed the clipboard and flipped over the paper on it to find some white space. I held up the paper for her to be able to write. Her first attempt was a mix of broken letters, indecipherable.

"I'm sorry, Cynthia, I don't know what you're trying to tell me."

I exchanged the clipboard for a laminated patient communication sheet showing common phrases and questions of critically ill patients.

I asked her to point to what was closest to what she wanted to say. She pointed to the picture of a family. "Would you like for us to call your family?" I inquired. "We don't have their information, but if you could write the number down, I'll give them a call and let them know what's happened."

I thought the tears welling up in her eyes were tears of joy. The joy of being reunited with her family. "Just point to the numbers corresponding to the phone number of the person you want me to call."

I held the sheet back up for her to see. She slowly started pointing but not at numbers. She selected five letters that broke my heart. N-O O-N-E. There was no one. The very first thing Cynthia wanted me to know was that she was alone. Illness has a way of making even the strongest person feel vulnerable. It's hard to hide much under those flimsy hospital gowns. It's rare to have someone who is already physically exposed willing to bare the hidden parts of their soul. The physical brokenness had also broken down the walls of ego. Brokenness is beautifully ugly, drawing to the surface everything ready to be pruned.

Seven days into her hospitalization, Cynthia was no longer confined to her room. Physical therapy had her up walking with support. She was an eager patient, anxious to get back on her feet. One day I commented, "You are doing great! You'll be back to your normal routine in no time."

This was when Cynthia began letting me into her story, her whole story, and the realization that she did not want to go back to how she used to be. One day I asked her what she thought about her accident. She closed her eyes for a moment but didn't respond. I pressed on. I asked if she saw the accident as something that had a purpose and not just a happenstance occurrence out of the cosmic blue. I wanted to know if she could see for herself the deeper purpose attached to the pains of life, the purpose attached to the trauma of change. She sat there thinking. Then she started sharing with me what her life looked like before the accident. She shared about the people who were in her life. She shared about the activities and things she loved. What she described wasn't memories of those people and events, but how she missed out on those experiences because she didn't have time. She shared what her life looked like trapped in a cycle of missed opportunities. She wasn't at a place where she could say the accident was a good thing, but she realized the accident did have meaning and purpose. It was being used in a manner she never expected. It caused her to pause in a way that she would have never agreed to. Nowhere on her agenda for this year did she have plans to spend a few weeks resting and recovering. But now she had an all-inclusive stay, confined to a building that smelled of antiseptic, surrounded by strangers, and having to relearn things she'd known her entire life, like walking. She also had to learn some new skills like how to trust, how to grow, and how to be at rest.

She confessed she had not realized how tired she had become and how much her lifestyle drained her. Despite how difficult everything had been over the past few weeks, she admitted she felt better than she'd ever felt in her entire life. She felt at peace, and that her life had gotten back on track. Sitting in her hospital room, she had time to dream again, time to allow a vision of her life to form and to allow herself to see the possibilities that surrounded her. She let out a small laugh. "Who knew that it would take something this drastic to wake me up?" she said.

I had to smile at that. The sacredness of rest remains even when we refuse to acknowledge it. The need to break away, for the body to have periods of peace, is rooted in our anatomy. We must have opportunities to heal. The mind must have a reprieve from thinking. The body needs rest from movement. Emotions need a release. The senses desire to be quieted. We need the social grace to find rest in another. Our soul yearns to soak in the created beauty around it, and our spirit calls for a relationship with the holy.

On the day she left the hospital, Cynthia left the staff a handwritten note. "Thank you. May I never forget the kindness you've shown, the love you've shared, or the care you've given. But most of all, may I never forget who I was when I was in your presence. You have made me better." Cynthia's words were for her medical team, but she echoed the heart's cry of many.

Healing occurs when we allow ourselves the time, space, and grace to be in the presence of God in the middle of our busy lives. What Cynthia was most thankful for wasn't anything that had to be done in a hospital. The hospital just happened to be the place where her life was revived. It was the place she found life-changing direction. In the middle of the messiness, in the middle of the trauma, in the middle of the pain, she found herself. The nurse who showed me the note had tears in her eyes. Cynthia was never alone on her journey; none of us are. We are all connected by our collective humanity. Sometimes the hard places have to be broken before we are willing to let others in.

Rest Is a Second Chance

Peace, understanding, and revelation came into that place for Cynthia. The place where our fear of being broken beyond repair meets our fear of staying the same. The place where things are hard and life gets difficult. Healing and wholeness require access into our lives, and room to make us better. That is what rest does. Rest causes you to be still and seek to know God. It calls for you to look deeper at yourself and your surroundings. It forces you to stop. We often view life as if looking through the window of a speeding car. Rest, rather, implores you to slow down and fully live. It challenges you to shift from having the scenery fly by in a blur to inhaling the scent of pine on the scenic route of your life. To take it all in and experience it. Rest is not simply pushing the pause button on your day. Rest is not merely taking a break. Rest is about replenishing, restoring, renewing, recovering, rebuilding, regenerating, remolding, and repairing. Rest begins with the prefix *re-* because it requires us to go back to a prior state. It is a second chance. It's an opportunity to put back in order anything that has shifted out of alignment with God's best.

Cynthia was too busy to rest, or so she had told herself. She refused to block off time for vacations. Rather than making room for the things she desired, she chose to fantasize about it. She opted to sacrifice her safety to take a mental reprieve each day. As she drove back and forth during the daily commute, she traded being alert on the busy interstates with time to zone out. The only mental break she found within her day, her only opportunity to unwind, came during a time when she needed to be on guard. Rest will win every battle you initiate with it. You can either honor your need for rest or surrender to the one-two punch of a mandatory rest.

Chronic insufficient rest ultimately leads to a rest deficit. This deficiency occurs when the amount of rest you get is inadequate to meet your daily energy expenditures. The law of conservation states that energy cannot be created or destroyed. It can only be converted to different forms or transferred. For every minute of activity, you are using energy. Daily, you transfer energy from your reservoir to your activity account and use it to live. The only way to replenish the energy lost is to receive a transfer of energy from another source. Rest is the conductor connecting you to the energy refill you need. The problem is, if you don't get the right kind of rest, you will still feel empty.

When I first realized there were different types of rest, I was captivated by the revelation. How can rest be complicated? Isn't resting supposed to be simple? So if it's so simple, why do so many of us have such a hard time doing it? And when we do it, why do we still not feel rested? These were the questions that led me on a quest to dig deeper, to uncover the hidden secrets of the well rested and to recline there in that knowledge until I too found room to breathe.

Just in reading this chapter, you have used physical, mental, emotional, spiritual, social, sensory, and creative energy. Each is drawing from a different energy pool. Each needs to be restored in preparation for the next time it will be called upon. Your body needs physical, mental, emotional, spiritual, social, sensory, and creative rest. Omit any one of these, and you will feel the consequences of the resulting rest deficit.

So what kind of tired are you?

If you awake full of energy every morning and are dragging by the afternoon, you may be missing adequate physical rest to sustain your day. If you get out of bed tired in the morning and then become energized as the day progresses, you may be experiencing creative restlessness. And if you experience an overall lack of meaning and fulfillment, a spiritual or emotional rest deficit may be to blame. Understanding which type of rest you are deficient in is critical to correcting this imbalance.

If your job is mentally draining but physically undemanding, physical rest will fail to leave you feeling rested. Mental rest is what's required to bring your mental reservoir back to a healthy level. If you spend most of your day staring at a bright computer screen or hearing constant noise, your body will need sensory rest to feel renewed. If your circumstances cause you to struggle with faith and the meaning of life, your soul will desire spiritual rest to return to a place of peaceful contentment.

For every depleting activity in your day, there is a counter reviving activity to balance the scales. Before we go any further, it's important you identify your rest deficits. Take a moment to go to the end of the book. Complete the personal rest deficit assessment you'll find there. Before you read the deeper discussion in the next seven chapters on each type of rest, it's important you take an introspective look at your current state. Doing so will allow you to see immediately which types of rest you need to focus on getting and which types you already excel at obtaining.

In the next chapters, I will discuss the seven types of rest using the R-E-S-T method:

- Recognize your risk
- Evaluate your current position
- Science and research
- Today's application

Each chapter will give you the key concepts relating to that specific type of rest. These chapters are purposefully concise and dense. Tired people don't have long attention spans, and this book was designed with you in mind. If you would like a more in-depth discussion on any specific type of rest, don't hesitate to reach out to me for more information. I want you to be successful at resting well.

You can either make time for rest or rest will take the time it needs. The choice is yours. The best time to rest is when you don't have time for it. Determine the rest you've been missing, and you will recover your life, renew your energy, and restore your sanity.

Chapter 4

Physical Rest

When You Lay Your Body Down

The body tells its story in stillness. When we are physically active, we focus on the motion without sensing the conversation going on inside of us. In stillness, we can recognize when movement is no longer serving us well. Injure a part of your body today and tomorrow you will feel the full extent of the damage done. This process of inner healing occurs daily in our health. When we stop long enough, we can feel the pull toward the natural cycle of rest. The body knows when there is an imbalance; we've just refused to trust it. Instead, we belittle its pleas and shut up its protests. We treat the vessel we need most to live like an optional asset. In the stillness, we fear what we will find, so we keep moving.

we do the same w/ Christ

I have a type A personality. I'm a gal with a plan, and I'm going to work my plan. Childbirth was just another opportunity to prove myself to myself. I don't know where we women get this idea that natural childbirth is a badge of honor. Who comes up with this stuff? But I drank the poison in one big gulp. I was going to show the world I was woman enough to push this baby out naturally without any medications or any assistance from doctors. I mean, who needs doctors anyway to birth babies? I had my birthing plan, and I was good to go. I'm reminded of the saying "<u>Man plans, God laughs.</u>"

My water broke one evening as I was reading about breastfeeding. I'm sure there is some medical connection there. I grabbed my bag, which had been sitting at the foyer door for two weeks. Yep, I was on it! I advised my husband to get ready to meet our son. The first contractions were no problem. I had this. Everything was on point with my birthing plan. I had copies for my husband, the nurses, and the doctor. For some reason, they did not look appreciative. My seasoned nurse gave me a saucy look. She sat my neatly organized plan on a shelf and went about the work of inserting IVs and attaching monitors. Four hours into labor the unthinkable happened. Pain seized my body in a way I didn't believe humanly possible, and I've spent years studying the body. Words like *escalating* took on new meaning. I had participated in numerous deliveries as a medical student, watching strong women transform before me as the contractions settled in. I secretly thought them wimpy. I repent for this misconception. They were simply authentic and real.

My eyes locked onto my now smiling nurse who bravely asked, "Now what does the plan say we do about this?" I won't repeat my reply, but let's just say it left no room for further snide remarks. I have a sweet spot for nurses. They are the backbone of medicine, but she was treading on unstable ground. A type A with no plan is like a beach with no sand. Moments later the anesthesiologist appeared in the room. He didn't mention my birthing plan. He went right to work relieving my pain.

I don't recall much afterward. The combination of drugs, the exhaustion, or both knocked me out. When I awoke, I found myself paralyzed from the neck down. My mouth was numb, and I couldn't feel my body, not a single muscle or nerve responded to my brain's commands. Panic occurs when your body refuses to obey. I saw my husband sitting on the side of the bed watching the monitors. It was just the two of us in the room—well, the three of us, including our unborn child. It was as if my husband could sense something wasn't right; his hands clasped around each other and his eyes darted between the baby's monitor and mine. I opened my mouth but nothing came out. My body chemically quieted to the point of nonresponse.

The monitor slowly decreased the frequency of the beeps. I heard it before I felt the sensation of drifting. The rhythmic tune of two hearts beating in one body started to fade. If help didn't come soon, I would die like my mother. She died soon after I was born, the cause of death unknown. Was this what happened? Did she have some unusual reaction to the anesthesia? I tried again to move. Nothing. I was numb from the neck down, including my lips. I did the only thing I could do; I started to pray. "God, don't let me die. Don't leave my husband to raise our child by himself. Help me give voice to what my body is feeling." I opened my mouth; the smallest little squeak came out, and it was sufficient. My husband turned and looked at me. Our eyes communed in a way that occurs only between two people who have shared soul to soul, who have learned to struggle together, laugh together, live together, love together, and fight together. I mouthed the words "Something is wrong. I can't move."

I spent the next minutes in and out of consciousness. The room filled with people checking me and reassuring us. The medications were reversed, after which my strength returned. My body awakened to the sensations of my nerves, muscles, and tissues. I was liberated to movement. The birth of my first son asked my body to accept a level of stillness that left me terrified. It robbed my ability to speak and to move freely. Ultimately, it hindered me from seeking rest and set me on a course to stay as active as possible.

In the years that followed, I resisted stillness. Stillness felt like a type of purgatory, a place of uncertainty and ambiguity. Not a destination to choose but one to be delivered unto. A prison for those it captured. It was a place to escape from, so I ran in the opposite direction. I ran toward a stuffed calendar, more deadlines, extra shifts, and a full agenda. Running is beneficial only if it takes you toward where you desire to be. I was off track and started looking for the arrows pointing me back on course. Those arrows directed me to an appreciation of my body's need for physical rest. Let's see what the R-E-S-T method reveals about your body's rest requirements.

Recognize Your Risk

There are both passive and active forms of physical rest. Passive physical rest is outside of your direct control. It feels like someone has flipped off a switch, forcing you to be still. Inertia is a healing place, where stillness leads to recovery of the body's natural ability to heal itself. Sleeping and napping are the two most common types of passive rest. Sleep is not an option. Whether or not you choose to lay your body down, eventually your body will shut down. Sleep is required for health. It is not the foundation of rest, but the by-product of rest. There are many good books on how to improve your sleep environment and practice good sleep hygiene habits. I don't want to spend my short time with you in this book discussing sleep. I want to make sure you know how to listen to your body so that your sleep will be sweet. Let's uncover the types of active physical rest you can enjoy to improve the quality of your passive rest.

The most effective forms of active physical rest include dynamic

stretching, breathing exercises, soaking baths, prayer walks, and ✳
stretching poses. These forms of active physical rest release the tension in muscle groups and restore calm to the body. If you use your
physical body throughout the day, you need physical rest. This is a
practice common to athletes. They are mindful to include stretching
after weight lifting or rest days after a demanding workout. But the
mom lifting a thirty-five-pound toddler a gazillion times a day rarely
thinks to stretch her arm and neck muscles.

The type of active rest required for you depends on your propen-
sity to carry stress in specific areas of your body. As you are reading,
what parts of your body do you sense most? Does your neck feel tense? neck.
Are your hands clenched around the book cover? Did you find your
toes curled up? Is there any pressure behind your eyes? Any sensation
of a headache brewing? Are you grinding your teeth? Do your facial
muscles feel strained? What is your body trying to tell you about the
rest it needs?

Communication is the lifeline of health. Long before your doctor,
your lab work, or any imaging studies can reveal an imbalance, your
body will begin to reveal these things to you. But the still small voice
inside cannot compete with the loud hum of your frantic schedule. To
hear the message your body is trying to deliver, you must first learn
how to listen to it once again.

I find children do a much better job at this than adults. It can be
tiresome when your little one is constantly showing you every bump,
every boo-boo, every bruise, every scratch, every little bit of nothing
they feel in their body. We tell him, "That's nothing, sweetheart. It's
just a bruise." And we teach her to ignore her body. We send the mes- |||
sage that feeling too much is weak and to acknowledge our body's
communication is wimpy. As the years pass, we try to improve our

bodies, to make them stronger, faster, and more powerful. We lift weights, and we do activities that strain and stress our bodies. We embrace "no pain, no gain" as the gospel truth.

All the while our bodies try to communicate. Twinges of communication butting against our shut-up-already attitude. When someone comes to me with chest pain they have had for months, or a yearlong cough or a golf-ball-sized breast tumor, I always ask why they waited so long for evaluation.

You can pretend like the need for rest somehow does not apply to you and your life, but your yawn tells a different story. It boggles my brain how little we trust our body to speak truth. The part of us that takes us into the world, shows us beauty, and gives us freedom to move is treated like an enemy. The vessel through which all our life occurs is undervalued to the point that we won't even allow ourselves a yearly physical—and we're proud of our ability to ignore and conceal.

So often we forget to trust in the Lord

Preventative medicine is the goal of modern health care, but it is not where we are currently. It seems easier to treat the illness after the fact, rather than doing something so you never reach that level of disease. Don't be deceived; there are no shortcuts to good health, but there are ways of getting there that will help you feel better faster.

Evaluate Your Current Position

The heat of the morning sun warms up the field. Dew glistens off the blades of grass, browning from the cool fall nights. Young legs run and jump on the field. Older legs settle into canvas yard chairs. At one corner of the field stands a sign with a list of reminders from your child: (1) I'M A KID. (2) IT'S JUST A GAME. (3) MY COACH IS A VOLUNTEER. (4) THE OFFICIALS ARE HUMAN. (5) AND LASTLY, NO COLLEGE SCHOLARSHIPS WILL BE PASSED OUT AT THE END OF TODAY'S GAMES.

Each is a needed reminder for parent and grandparent fans to stay civil when the games begin. This is the life of the youth soccer family.

On this particular day, my son's team was in the Pappy Dunn tournament. They have fought hard during their qualifying game, outplaying and outlasting many teams to make it to the semifinals. Every player arrived ready to give 100 percent. Every player showed up wanting a piece of the action. Throughout the season their coach had focused on honing skills over banking wins, but he had made it clear that this was not a regular game. Everyone would not be getting equal play time. The goal was to win. The star players graced the fields eager to battle for their position in the finals. I probably should have been focusing on my son on the field, but my gaze locked on one young man sitting on the sidelines. He was a good solid player but not considered one of the stars. This did not change his outlook on who he was or his passion for helping his team. From my seat I could read his lips: "Coach, put me in."

The kids played a fast-paced full-on game. By the half, we were up 5–0. Players dragged themselves off the field and collapsed onto the bench. Both sides of the field were feeling the strain of this battle, but none of the players were willing to relent their position. Each reassured the coach, "I don't need a break. I can keep going." Their heart and spirit forgot to check in with the body responsible for actually doing the work. The middle of the second half told the truth of their predicament. Our players were out of juice. Our 5–0 lead dropped to 5–3 within the last five minutes of the game. Pride and the inability to let others step into their moment of opportunity was threatening to cost us the game. My sideline buddy was unfazed and still chanting, "Let me in, Coach!" This time the coach heard him.

There are those who are naturally gifted and those who are not but make up what they lack in ability with passion. Each great team needs this combination to succeed. At the water break, the coach exchanged many of our elite players for our passionate players, and with this change came a wind of revival. By refreshing the field with well-rested players, the coach ensured that the other team had no chance. We didn't score any more points, but neither did the other team. The bleeding stopped, and we went on to the finals. When our fresh second-string players took the field, they brought with them the power of being well rested. They brought a burst of energy the other team could not match. They did not have the skills of those they were playing against, but what they lacked in skill they made up in pure adrenaline. The other team's coach resisted exchanging his elite players. He was convinced skill would be enough; thankfully we were willing to bring in rest.

None of us are at our best when depleted. Our bodies cannot fully function when they are in a constant fight for excellence, high-performance, maximum effectiveness, and optimal capacity. The effects of the fight will ultimately be known. It's time to transition from our daily hustle to daily hush. In the hush, tension releases and recovery begins. Consider how different activities affect your body. The chemicals released during activities have an effect on your muscles, nervous system, circulatory system, and respiratory system.

Which activities cause you to feel energized? What habits create a sense of calm and relaxation?

Make an effort to find what restores you. Experiment with types of active physical rest to see which produce a deeper level of restfulness, peace, and well-being. What you do *to* your body and what you do *with* your body must balance to maintain equilibrium. We have to stop acting like honoring our body's physical needs is a sign of weakness. Rethink your position on body care. You may feel like a warrior battling for all you hold dear, but even warriors analyze their position. Whether you are a prayer warrior, love warrior, hope warrior, peace warrior, or a just-trying-to-make-it-through-the-day warrior, all warriors must know what weapons they have at their disposal. Rest is a time-tested weapon that can help you be victorious in battle.

Here are some signs you might be suffering from a physical rest deficit:

- You lack the energy needed to do all of the physical tasks on your to-do list.
- You feel tired but have difficulty falling asleep.
- You have a weak immune system with frequent colds and illnesses.
- You experience frequent muscle pain and soreness.
- You depend on substances to give you more energy (caffeine, energy bars, sugar).
- You depend on substances to give you more rest (alcohol, pills, comfort foods).

Science and Research

In a survey conducted by the National Sleep Foundation, 60 percent of the participants reported they had trouble sleeping almost every night, with over 40 percent stating they rarely got a good night's sleep.[1] For years, researchers have been searching for ways to help us sleep better. We have spent a lot of time and energy on sleep, and we have disconnected the vital relationship between sleep and rest. In doing so, we have dismissed the effects of our lifestyle on our ability to enjoy passive and active physical rest.

Studies reveal one-third of the population feels worn out because of our overbooked lives. A staggering 97 percent of us state we feel tired most of the time, and my medical colleagues state that over 10 percent of those visiting their offices are there for the purpose of investigating their unexplained fatigue. As a result, the sales of supplements such as energy drinks, protein bars, and ginseng have shot up more than 5 percent in the past two years as we battle exhaustion.[2] The answer isn't in a quick fix, but in routinely giving your body the types of active rest it thrives on.

At my alma mater, the University of Georgia, a study showed exercising lightly three days a week for just twenty minutes reduced fatigue symptoms by 65 percent and led to participants feeling more energized after six weeks.[3] The effects of regular exercise to increase blood flow to the heart and improve oxygen delivery to the lungs also revived the body's ability to supply nutrients throughout the body. Next time you're tempted to grab a can of Red Bull, force yourself outside for a ten- to twenty-minute walk. Instead of experiencing the highs and lows of artificial stimulants, you'll feel the sustained alertness of a body under restoration.

I challenge you to be brave enough to listen to what your body is saying and respond by rectifying any problems you find. Learn to speak your body's love language. Listen to the unspoken language of your muscles and nerves, then speak back in a language it understands. If your muscles are tight because you hold stress in your body, then speak the language of release by alternating rhythmic stretching and stretching poses. If your nerve endings are irritated and inflamed, speak back by increasing the blood flow throughout your body with walking and light aerobic activity. The increased circulation will take disease-fighting, inflammation-reducing cells to the places in need of healing. These healing cells are already inside of you, but they can reach injured areas only when your circulatory system is activated. A fifteen-minute leisure or prayer walk during your morning or afternoon break could be the difference between a tension headache and a pain-free day. We confuse the exercise recommended for weight loss with the activities promoting body peace. Exercise for weight loss is often a physical stressor to the body. It is a good form of stress, yet all stress needs a reprieve. Even the most trained athlete learns periodic rest improves the outcome of their physical endurance activities.

Today's Application

Desperation can make you do strange things like show up for a five a.m. relaxation class. On one particular morning I found myself in a room full of other desperate people lying facedown on a foam mat trying to breathe without snorting. For those of us with a hint of belly flab, trying to inhale air while gravity pushes on the gut is challenging. Lying prone is uncomfortable. It's a vulnerable position for the body to be in, and it's a vulnerable position for our ego. It requires our participation in a way that pulls us back from frantic activity and implores us to settle down. It's like a time-out for grown-ups, and nobody likes time-outs.

Time-out is not always a punishment. Sometimes it's the way a good parent encourages a break from the activity that is causing destructive results. This time-out was one I needed. It was taking me back to an understanding of my body and relearning what it needed. It was showing me how to restore my relationship with time. If our bodies had their way, they would slip into these time-outs without argument or preamble. They would lay themselves down on purpose, knowing greater is the reward of having willingly gone into the resting place. Our bodies hold knowledge we refuse to heed. Our bodies know secret paths into sacred rest if only we are willing to listen to them. Life is not all about the doing; it's about the being, the seeing, the knowing, and the experiencing. All of these life gems are found when we lay ourselves down.

Practice Body Fluidity—When you are awake, don't stay in the same position for more than an hour. You are not dead yet. Keep your body flexible and in gentle motion. Periodically today stretch or roll your head in circles. Curl and uncurl your toes. Open and close your mouth. Rock back on your heels, then rock forward to stand on your toes. Squeeze and open your hands. These small acts of motion will help prevent stiffness from setting in.

Give Stillness Purpose—Choose to be still on purpose for five minutes while lying down. Supine or prone—it's your choice. Pick which feels right for you today. Purposely use the time to focus on how your body feels. Is something hurting? If so, inquire why. Are you taking deep breaths or shallow breaths? In Genesis, God breathed life into man. Often in our rush, we transition from taking full breaths to taking short panting breaths. We stop inhaling the holy and instead learn to rely on our own vapor. Breathe in deeply and with each breath remember who is breathing into you. Receive the well-rested life He is offering.

Prepare for Sleep—Develop a bedtime routine to prepare your body for sleep. If you find water to be calming, take a bath or shower before you turn in for the night. Slip into something comfortable to signal to your body it's bedtime. Dim the lights. Avoid loud sound and the flashing lights of your TV screens.

Resist the temptation to check your social media accounts or your text messages. Spend a few moments doing stretching poses to relax the muscles you've been using all day. Get into bed around the same time each night so that your body can begin to trust you to provide it with the rest it needs.

Chapter 5

Mental Rest

Quiet Cerebral Background Noise

The desk in my home office is the place I store papers, office supplies, and important documents. The filing system separates the important from the trivial. The kid's construction paper, scissors, and coloring markers remain a safe distance from our passports and tax documents. Recently we decided to redo the office. Five hours of sorting and ten trash bags later, I was seriously contemplating volunteering to be on an episode of *Hoarders*. When left unchecked, clutter happens. Your mind is no different. It can hold an inconceivable amount of information. It is also able to file, sort, and arrange information effectively. The life-changing power of tidying up your mind starts with letting go of those thoughts that are not producing a positive effect in your life.

As important as it is to rest your body, it's equally important to quiet your mind from the ongoing influx of information it receives. Much like our social media news feeds, our mental background noise is often infused with negativity. Thoughts about the future are contaminated with anxiety, thoughts about the past are tainted with regret, and thoughts about the present are spoiled with discontentment.

The mind is magnificent, but it has its own agenda. Rather than willingly focusing on positive affirming thoughts, the mind prefers to settle upon negative ones that intensify stress, worry, anger, and frustration. It will attempt to occupy your attention with useless information, depleting your time and your energy. Mental rest involves relinquishing the constant stream of thoughts entering your mind quickly and obtaining a sense of cerebral stillness.

In the cerebral realm, your brain is under the influence of constant background noise. Your mind chatter may seem like it never stops. We are endlessly contemplating ideas, thoughts, feelings, and emotions. Trying to clear your mind of this background noise can be difficult. Just when you think you've quieted your mind, suddenly another thought dances across your mental space. These thoughts can be desirable and motivating, or they can be untamed and chaotic. All become part of your background noise and influence your day.

Cerebral background noise is the ongoing chatter of the mind. It's the internal running commentary you have with yourself. It's the white space of the brain where your ideas are born and your feelings roam freely. It plays from the moment you wake up in the morning to the moment you fall asleep at night. It can even prevent you from falling asleep. You may be unaware of this mental noise because it can become a natural part of your life. My mental noise will sound different from your mental noise, but both have the potential to be draining and exhausting.

Types of mental noise can include the following:

- self-critiquing and evaluating with an ongoing inner monologue
- thinking the same thoughts over and over as if stuck in an endless loop
- reliving past events and rewriting your script with what you wish you'd done or said

- dwelling on what-ifs and fearing the future
- judging and processing current situations against the measuring stick of a past pain or regret
- constant escapism—fantasizing about another place/time instead of experiencing the present
- continuously running inner commentary that disturbs peace of mind
- never being totally present—always thinking about something other than what's in front of you

Wouldn't it be great if you could achieve a state where you could think when you need to, like solving a problem or making a plan, and then after that just switch off the mind? Let's apply the R-E-S-T method to looking at how you can quiet your cerebral background noise.

Recognize Your Risk

Mental fatigue results when overactivity of the brain leads to the brain cells becoming exhausted. The continued mental effort required to perform tasks and the concentration demands on your mind predispose those with creative, academic, and mentally stressful jobs to this type of rest deficit. The signs of mental exhaustion are often worse later in the workday as the stimulation from your morning caffeine lessens. Mind fog rolls in and with it reduced concentration, lack of focus, increased mistakes, poor memory recall, a decreased ability to solve problems, and more difficulty completing what you need to get done. The temptation is to jolt your brain to attention with more stimulants. Unfortunately, every trip up the roller coaster must come down.

If left unchecked, mental fatigue can worsen to mental diseases like depression. Those with a mental rest deficit often experience brain chatter

BRITT

BRITT

while asleep and never feel at peace. Stressors from the day can remain in the brain's stream of consciousness and be carried over into sleep, keeping the mind active when it should be at rest. A purging of the mind before turning in for the night is needed to declutter your mental space.

Evaluate Your Current Position

Mental rest reminds me of a story of two men who ran into a young woman struggling to cross a river. Fearful of the current, she asked if they could carry her across. One of the men hesitated because of his religious beliefs. The other quickly picked her up onto his shoulders and carried her across to the other side. She thanked him, and they went their separate ways. As the men continued on their way, the one who had declined to offer help was restless and brooding.

Eventually, he could no longer hold his thoughts to himself, saying, "We are taught to avoid any contact with women, but you picked that one up on your shoulders and carried her!"

The second man replied, "My friend, I set her down on the other side hours ago, yet you are still carrying her."

Like the indignant man in the story, we hold on to some mental baggage past its expiration date. Don't allow your mind to keep you from being present in the current moment. You can shift where you place your attention and meditate on those things that produce good fruit in your life.

What thoughts do you carry unnecessarily?

Here are some signs you might be suffering from a mental rest deficit:

- You feel as if you can't keep up mentally with your to-do list.
- You experience irritation or frustration when thinking about your day.

- You avoid some activities because you fear you will make an error.
- You feel drowsy or as if you are in a mental fog during the day.
- You snap at your family and coworkers about insignificant things.
- You spend most of your day on tasks you find overwhelming.

Science and Research

Mental fatigue is one of the significant causes of avoidable accidents. When the mind is tired, it no longer has the capacity to effectively control the body and reflexes. The result includes increased falls, car accidents, and damaging mistakes. Studies evaluating the brain's activity before and after mind-taxing activities reveal a drop in electrical brain impulses following these activities. The decreased energy was positively associated with a decrease in the ability to perform future tasks.[1] Most of our to-do lists are not limited to purely mental jobs, but those that require both our mind and body. A 2015 study showed that when we attempt mental and physical tasks at the same time, we activate specific areas of our brain called the prefrontal cortex. Because of this activation, our bodies become fatigued much sooner than if we were solely participating in a physical task.[2] The mind in effect is accelerating the depletion of our physical energy. If the mind can deplete you physically, it stands to reason the reverse can be true: You can be physically strengthened by the renewal of your mind.

Today's Application

Your brain is constantly working overtime to conquer your never-ending to-do list, and it deserves a rest. Mental rest is your mind's comfort zone. It's the place your brain retreats to feel safe, so your mind can function optimally. There is no quick fix for a chronic mental rest deficit. It results from daily draining your reserves and requires a daily commitment to restore the mind to a place of restfulness. The most valuable thing you can do for your sanity is to let your mind rest and allow room for the regeneration of what's being depleted every day. Here are some tips you can begin using today to clear your mental fog and settle your mind.

Time Block Low-Yield Activities—Review how you spend your time and how you feel mentally after different activities. Isolate those activities that fail to yield consistent positive gains and determine their place in your life. Eliminate activities you no longer find value in. Consider scheduling limited time blocks for those activities you must complete. Do them all at once, preferably early in the day when your mind is most clear. Thirty minutes is a good duration to start with for each time block. Depending on your career and responsibilities, you may need more than one time block for the same energy-draining tasks. You will prevent recurrent fluctuations of your think tank as you limit your daily exposure to these activities. Some activities that do best in time blocks include managing email, engaging in social media, completing menial office tasks, surfing the internet, video gaming, watching television, and catching up on current news events.

Meditate—Spend a few moments right now to observe what thoughts are occupying your mind. Don't analyze them, judge them, or try to understand them. Simply start by acknowledging you have them. You may find images and situations entering your brain space you had no idea were there. Reclaim your mental territory. An excellent mental rule to practice is in Philippians 4:8, where we are encouraged to allow our thoughts to rest on whatever is true, whatever is noble, whatever is right, whatever is pure, whatever is lovely, whatever is admirable—if anything is excellent or praiseworthy—think about such things. Make a conscious effort to fill your mental space with restorative thoughts.

Create a Mental Sanctuary—When everything in your day looks like chaos, where will your mind retreat for order? The mind must have a place to rest, and that place must be sacred. Your brain and neurons are wired to fight for your life. They are daily on alert looking for potential dangers. Your mind is sacrificial. It does not seek rest because it loves protecting your body more than it values itself. Mental rest will require your mind to let down its guard. Romans 8:6 warns that to set the mind on the flesh (temporal gratification of your senses) is death, but to set the mind on the spirit (eternal gratification of your soul) will bring life and peace. This is a life-changing equation. A mind set on habitually practicing stress and striving to satisfy your desires ends in death. A mind set on habitually practicing the ways of God leads to life and peace. One way to create a mental sanctuary is to choose a characteristic of God to rest on each day like love, joy, peace, kindness, goodness, gentleness, and faithfulness. Let each characteristic be the mental place you return to throughout the day as you practice creating a mental sanctuary.

Chapter 6

Emotional Rest

Acknowledge Your Current Truth

I often dress in layers when speaking at events. You never know if conference rooms will be northern cold or southern hot. This room was in a downtown Philadelphia hotel, and they were serious about keeping their decorative ice sculptures intact. My light jacket was a fitting barrier from the chilled temperatures but did little to warm the cool expressions on the faces in the room.

After introductions I climbed the side stairs to the stage. My Power-Point was queued, and my mic was ready, but I was frozen. This was not my first rodeo. It was more of an encore presentation. I had been the keynote speaker at the Women in Medicine conference the year prior. These ladies had invited me back this year for the national event. Their response to my challenging talk encouraging them to resist hiding behind their white coats had been incredible. I had implored them to be real and relevant in their interactions with others and to be real with themselves about what they needed to enjoy this life they created. These women were up to the challenge. They were looking for authenticity and hungry for accountability.

This year the event planners had asked me to lead a special session they had never attempted before. My task was to lead these women into a time of fellowship and small group discussion on the issues affecting their lives. Girl talk on the veranda as we lounged in deck chairs sharing about our real lives and real struggles as women in medicine. It sounded simple enough in the email invitation. In a ministry setting, this really would have been easy. But in a room full of surgeons, internists, obstetricians, gynecologists, dentists, medical students, residents, and psychiatrists, not so much. As I looked out into their faces, it hit me that these women were comfortable behind their emotional walls. Years of residency and medical school had taught them you don't bring your emotions to the table. What a flawed system. Its teachings make our healers even more vulnerable to the attacks of emotional pain.

Just like these healers, some of you have been trained to shelve your emotions. You bottle up your feelings and place them on a high shelf. Then you leave them there as if they don't exist. But they do. Shelved emotions are the rawest kind. They are not tempered by exposure and are easily bruised on contact. So contact becomes the enemy, and we cocoon in our isolation. We limit the ability to use our emotions for our own healing. Emotions are powerful. They can override thoughts, influence our relationships, and transform our behavior. They empower us to understand ourselves and overcome challenges. Emotions are to be explored, encountered, and enjoyed. They were never meant to be bottled up.

As I stepped onto the stage at the Women in Medicine conference, I knew my prepared speech wasn't going to accomplish the job. Pretty choreographed words can never dance passionately enough to shake loose what's hiding on the top shelf. Talk about a scary moment, standing before hundreds of your peers with no idea of your next move.

I caught the eye of one of the ladies I had spoken with at breakfast. We had sipped our coffee and munched on pastries over a revealing conversation about feeling alone in our respective hospitals. We were unable to give voice to the stress for fear of appearing weak. Unwilling to seek out assistance for fear of being deemed incapable. Striving and pushing ourselves to our emotional limits. Yet here we were seated together in the City of Brotherly Love still afraid to share our common frailties, afraid to reveal our truth to those most likely to understand.

It was time to address the elephant sitting in the front row.

"Greetings, ladies. I've been charged with the task of leading us into a time of sisterhood. When we leave this room, we will be sharing a meal together. Then we will convene outside in groups of six to eight to share and receive from each other through a series of discussion questions. Unless something changes right now, we will not be successful in completing this task. It's not because you are incapable of doing it. It's because we, the collective medical teaching body, have shamed you into avoidance. Let me be the first to apologize. As an instructor and clinical advisor, I am sorry for contributing to the system that has hardened you. As a medical student, we chastised you when the first tears fell at the loss of a patient. In residency, we pushed you to ignore the emotions of others so they would not pollute your ability to get the job done. And now we see you weary, tired, and broken, and we ask you to open up so we can help you heal. Forgive us for what we have done. I'm tired of acting like things don't bother me, and I believe you are too. Let's just be real. Let's talk about our marriages that are struggling because we've forgotten how to be loved. Let's share about our kids who we fear will resent us for making sure their financial needs were met but not their relational needs. Lay down the heaviness and leave here this weekend lighter and freer."

In the silence that followed, I could hear the sound of vessels cracking as they fell low. Bottled-up emotions flowed free. My impromptu speech was not those exact words because, well, it was impromptu, but close enough. It was a million miles from the talk I had prepared, but it was the catalyst for a tangible shift in the atmosphere. Many began to cry. Deep relief coming in waves of pent-up grief. Some joined hands with the woman beside her. Some sat in shock. Locked in the moment, unsure what to do, say, or feel. It was a shattering of the norm, and it shook loose everything that was not grounded in truth.

That afternoon we rested in each other. We shared about those times when we mourned a loss, and we shared about why we are driven to do what we do. A cornucopia of board-certified, highly trained, and highly accomplished women of every race and religion learned the meaning of emotional rest that day.

Recognize Your Risk

You experience emotional rest when you no longer feel the need to perform or meet external expectations. It is the cessation of emotional striving. We each have an internal capacity to manage emotions. We pour out of this space as we offer sympathy to a friend who just lost her husband, console a tearful toddler in our arms, or encourage our coworker on a job well done. Each interaction is giving a bit of ourselves. When our emotional withdrawals exceed our emotional capacity, we will experience emotional fatigue. Emotional rest is a deposit back into our emotional account.

Where are you expending emotional energy? In an angry outburst during your morning commute? With anxious thoughts while watching the evening news? Being depressed about the climbing number on the scale? In a conflict at work? While parenting a toddler, tween, teen, or graduate? Regardless of the outlet, you are regularly using your emotions to interact with those around you.

Emotions are similar to infections; they are highly contagious. As you share your emotions, you are also being affected by the emotions of others. When in proximity to others, emotions will spread. Now with the vast accessibility of the internet, they can be spread directly or indirectly. Face-to-face conversations are now less important, as text messages, phone calls, Periscope videos, Facebook posts, tweets, and emails give us opportunities to share our emotions at any time, day or night. We are more emotionally connected to the world than ever before, and because of this fact, we have tapped out our emotional capacity.

I fear we have lost our ability to process our emotions. It is easier to participate in an emotional rant on social media than to process why that pain of rejection is there in the first place. It's simpler to send an email than to stop by to visit the friend who just lost his job. Face-to-face interaction leaves no place to hide. Your body language communicates your current emotional state, and you may not welcome that communication because your current emotional state may be very different from the social media blast you would rather share. Technology has made it easy to *act* like we have our act together.

My youngest son enjoys acting and theater. I can often find him rewatching a favorite TV show and repeating the actors' lines word for word. When he goes into character, he becomes a different person. The facial expressions are not his own. His voice is different, and his mannerisms are that of the character he is portraying.

Are there times you find yourself performing? Have you ever met someone who acts like a totally different person depending on their surroundings? They may be insecure around their coworkers and an extroverted comedian with their friends. They may appear to seek approval from their boss and be judgmental with their spouse. You could be enjoying lunch with them and suddenly they change their behavior the moment someone new joins the table.

Do you find you act differently when around certain people? If so, you are in good company. Most successful people admit they have different personas in different situations. This is not a condemnation for not being authentically you 100 percent of the time. The truth is that we all have had moments of inauthenticity. We all feel the pressure to perform. This drive can be present in careers, family matters, and social relationships. It becomes engrained in our way of interacting with others to the extent we no longer feel comfortable being ourselves. We worry people won't get us or that we aren't good enough. So it feels safer showing up as the person we think everyone will like than to risk rejection. When we cease to be authentic, we dive deep into an emotional pit. The only way out is to return to the place where we can rest in our current truth without shame or guilt.

Evaluate Your Current Position

I cannot blame them for wanting better. Who doesn't want the good life? So when given the opportunity to advance in knowledge and to advance their position, Adam and Eve took it. They didn't consult their pastor. They didn't pray about it. They didn't Google it. No, they did what on the surface looked like a great move. Unbeknownst to them, that one decision would change everything.

It started in a relationship. Hearts connected over walks in the cool of the day. They shared conversations in earnest, equal parts listening, learning, and loving. Then came the silence. After one fatal decision, authenticity no longer felt safe.

"Adam, where are you?" He called into the hushed garden.[1]

"I was ashamed, so I hid from you," came the wounded reply.

A few pages into the story and the emotional masks are already in place. Emotional unrest leads to increased fear, shame, and desire to hide our current truth. We are skilled at hiding, even when we want to be found. Behind the bushes and the trees, Adam searched for safety. It was not there. He was in need of a place to rest. Hiding looks like rest. It shields, protects, and covers. But unlike rest, hiding drains. It pulls apart and separates. Rest rejoins. It is a reunion with your best self. You, before the hiding. You, before the shame.

Authenticity is living and behaving in a way that is consistent with your core values, desires, strengths, and weaknesses. It's being real about your current state of affairs. It's you telling your current truth. It is independent of the external influences of what others think and their power to manipulate your personal response to situations.

Here are some signs you might be suffering from an emotional rest deficit:

- You have a tendency to focus on your failures and flaws.
- You experience self-doubt and insecurity, which prevent you from trying new things.
- You constantly compensate for who you are with apologies or clarifications.
- You beat yourself up when you make even the slightest mistake.
- You feel depressed or angry when you think about your life.
- You exhibit excessive worrying or display feelings of anxiety about situations.

Science and Research

Do you know someone who is a chronic complainer or consistently pessimistic? How do you feel around them? Are you able to maintain your emotional ground or do you too begin with your own list of complaints?

The reciprocal effect of emotions has been widely studied. Psychologists describe emotional contagion as "the tendency to automatically mimic and synchronize expressions, vocalizations, postures, and movements with those of another person and, consequently, to converge emotionally."[2] We unconsciously and automatically mimic the emotional expressions of others. When someone smiles at us, we smile back. If we see someone crying, we are likely to experience sadness or empathy. The emotional expression of others triggers reactions in our brains, which lead us to draw upon our memories of when we last experienced that feeling. This predisposition to empathize can cause us to mistakenly interpret those feelings as our own, leaving us vulnerable to catch the emotions of the people we are around.

Feeling down? Spend a few minutes around someone with an infectious smile and a jovial disposition to help lift your feelings. Unfortunately, the same is true for negative emotions. Time spent in the company of someone dealing with depression can be a downer.

Research shows we have mirror neurons that trigger us to directly experience the emotional atmosphere of others.[3] Our emotional connectedness is an adaptation for our collective benefit. It puts the "human" back in *humanity*. It enables us to be compassionate. It's the force behind our urge to encourage the brokenhearted, console the hurting, and support those who are less fortunate. This emotional connectedness has a powerful impact on our relationships with our family, friends, and business associates. Over time our constant emotional exposure can lead to emotional fatigue: anxiety, irritability, depression, anger, apathy, and a loss of passion.

What effect does being in a constant state of emotional connectedness have on you? Research shows that introverts are more likely to be affected by others' positive emotions whereas extroverts tend to be more affected by others' negative emotional expressions. Women tend to be vulnerable to absorbing the stress and negativity of those around them.[4] Girls are often socialized to attend to the emotional needs of those they love. I was reminded of this fact this Christmas. I asked my niece what she wanted Santa to bring her and she animatedly described a baby doll who cries, pees, and poops. Does a seven-year-old need to be concerned with such things?

Men are not immune to emotional fatigue, but they are often more comfortable being their authentic selves. A group of men competing in a burping contest is evidence of this uncanny comfort level with self-exposure—the good, the bad, and the ugly. However, in marriage and fatherhood, the investment in emotional connectedness is much greater, and in these areas, many men feel the effects of a chronic emotional rest deficit.

Today's Application

We often don't realize how much our emotions are influenced by the emotional states of others. An important question to ask is: "In what direction are my emotions being influenced when I'm around someone else?" Pay close attention to your feelings in different settings and when around different people. Take an inventory of the people in your life who drain you and those who refresh you. Then take the initiative to end or limit toxic relationships and intentionally surround yourself with those who have a positive effect on your life.

Be Emotionally Aware—If you go to work in a good mood, only to find that by lunch you are feeling depressed, that's a strong indication you are encountering negative emotions in your workplace. If you feel anxious when around a friend and you find your mood improving when you're away from that person, it's time to evaluate the effect that relationship is having on your emotional health. As you begin paying attention to these clues, you will learn how to give and receive in your relationships in a way that leaves you emotionally healthy.

Cease Comparisons—Children don't use emotional masks. They don't have to resist the temptation to hide their true self. Their feelings are a part of who they are, and they are comfortable displaying everything they feel. It isn't until they start comparing themselves with others that the inauthenticity begins. Comparisons limit individuality and destroy the ability to be authentic. Trying to fit in is emotionally taxing. It's time to stop hustling for your worthiness. Instead, rest in the self-awareness of your unique quirks and propensities. Today think of two to three situations where you find yourself being inauthentic or performing too much to please others. What about yourself are you compensating for with inauthenticity? Acknowledge those areas and give yourself permission to cease comparing.

Risk Vulnerability—When we conceal our truth, we only hurt ourselves. We deplete our emotional capacity in the day-to-day task of living a lie. Emotional exposure is risky, but it's necessary to live fully. Risk being real; risk being vulnerable. Lean into the uncertainty of authenticity. Reacquaint yourself with the adventurer inside you. We are created to thrive in connection with others. Who are those people you most feel like yourself around? Open yourself to regular communion with the bread of self-disclosure and the wine of community. In drinking deeply in these rewarding relationships, you will find the strength to risk vulnerability with others.

Chapter 7

Spiritual Rest

Enter Your Personal Sanctuary

As a young child growing up without a mother, I believed God could not be trusted. Every relationship from that stage on was built upon a framework of guarded pain. Sometimes you have to wonder at God's divine plan. Someone holding on to deep pain is not who *I* would lead to be a healer. But, as He would have it, he led me into a profession based on healing. On the wall of my medical office in the place where the plaques, certificates, and accolades hang should hang a huge neon sign flashing WOUNDED HEALER.

What do you do when you look in the eyes of someone who has just told you they want to die? How do you help someone whose world you just rocked with a cancer diagnosis? What hope do you have to offer the paraplegic? What peace is there to give the mother holding a stillborn child? How do you comfort the uncomfortable? How do you ease the burdened?

These were some of the hardest questions I'd ever faced. And they were questions the people I counseled wanted answers to, answers I had no ability to give. I had no faith in God, and I did not believe in His promises. I could not see the evidence of who He said He was active and alive within my life or theirs. My spiritual journey was never about finding God. My journey has always been about finding home—a place of rest.

Home. I always knew even as a little girl that somewhere a place exists where my heart can rest in the comfortable armchair of life and recline into the soft contours of contentment and peace. Somewhere sits a fire lit by the heat of my past mistakes and fanned by the purity of a grace I've yet to fully grasp. Somewhere out there is the road that will lead me back to the home my spirit longs for, a place I left so long ago I can no longer tell if it truly existed or if it was only an illusion. A place secured by God's love and upheld by His peace.

The journey home did not take me past rainbows and sunsets. The road was more roller coaster than carousel, more tugboat than luxury cruise liner. There was no fanfare, no celebration along the way. No one cheered or gathered to congratulate me for the journey. There was no medal at the end of the marathon race toward the place of my longing. The course did not move me along like a raft drifting down the calm waters of a country stream. Rather, the journey home was a leap, a tandem leap from healing bridge to healing bridge.

Bridges are an interesting thing. They are a pathway connecting two places, often over an obstacle or tumultuous area. In many cases, we would never be able to cross wide gaps in the terrain while traveling without the assistance of bridges. When you are standing at the edge of a thorny embankment looking down at the raging waters below, dreaming about the inviting gardens on the other side can seem like a lost cause unless there is a bridge to join where you are presently at with where you desire to be.

Just as a structural bridge is needed to traverse natural ravines, metaphorical bridges are needed to traverse spiritual ravines. When deep pain enters your life, it can cut into your emotions, into your faith, and into your ability to trust God, creating a deep spiritual valley, a valley so expansive and so consuming it can become a refuge. It can become a place you can retreat for fear of being hurt again. I call this place the Valley of the Wounded, and I spent much of my childhood wandering around exploring what little it had to offer. I must admit it did offer protection because my pain was a barrier to building relationships with others who could potentially cause me future pain. It offered safety since few were willing to visit me in my place of discontentment. And it offered the needed motivation to excel at being self-sufficient and self-serving.

Ultimately, its offerings failed to meet what my heart and soul truly craved. It could never feel like home. It could never be my sanctuary.

We all need sanctuary, a secure place where protection reigns and comfort is received. We need relief from the daily struggles and times of immunity from outside attacks. Sanctuary is not simply a place; it's a state of being. There we find a sense of security and peace that flows from our connection to God. Sanctuary is where we lay down our fight and rest. In the process, we find our way back home to a relationship with God. This is the journey that rescued me from myself and wooed me back into the arms of God.

I spent a lot of time in college studying world religions in my search for truth. I didn't go looking for salvation, or Jesus, or God. I went looking to find what was missing in my life and I was open to whatever that looked like. I did not expect it to resemble a two-thousand-year-old Messiah. Despite my fight with the person of Jesus, the historical proof of his existence satisfied my mind. It was years later before my heart was ready for a relationship. The pain my heart had experienced was too fragile for the bigness of God. I couldn't fathom the gentleness behind such contained power.

Recognize Your Risk

"If you mention Jesus, I'm leaving."

It was a typical workday at the office. I had spent the better part of the morning treating patients with common internal medicine issues. Diabetes, hypertension, asthma, and heart disease were the illnesses of the day until she walked in. A new patient referred by a friend who thought I could help her. I wasn't two minutes into my initial interview questions when she made the above statement.

I am a Christian, but I don't make it a habit of quoting Bible verses or preaching while practicing medicine. My faith is a part of who I am. To deny its influence in my life would be inauthentic. Its effect in my life reaches into every interaction in how it prepares me to receive others. Faith preps my heart to care. In health care, caring is a good thing. Years of dealing with death, pain, and disease can leave you hardened and emotionally dry. Faith waters the parched ground, softening the soil and readying it for the seeds to be sown.

Seeds fall daily. Sometimes the field of my soul is ready to hold tight to this gift. At other times the seeds fall along my path, and I step over them as I rush by. Sometimes the seeds are totally destroyed by the fire arising from my burned-out life. Still, the gardener continues throwing these seeds, daily offering opportunities to let life go deep, daily revealing truths about the nature and character of God, daily unraveling my misconceptions about separation of faith and science.

Years into my medical training one of my professors warned us to avoid mixing faith with medical science. Regrettably, that professor died young. I hope somewhere along his journey someone was courageous enough to share their faith with him. He had been dangerously wrong in his assessment of faith and medicine.

A healer once made the profound statement, "One should not set about treating the body without the soul. This is exactly why most ailments are beyond the capabilities of Greek healers: they neglect the whole when that is what they should be paying attention to."[1]

You are made up of a body, a mind, and a spirit. Three unique parts make the whole. Whole is what your body thrives to become. Your body seeks to remember its disjointed relationship with your mind and spirit, and in doing so remember the sanctity of wholeness. It would stand to reason, however, if you can be whole, then you can also be the opposite of whole. You can be fragmented or broken. *Merriam-Webster*'s online dictionary defines *broken* as "violently separated into parts: shattered"; "damaged"; "disrupted by change"; "made weak or infirm"; "cut off: disconnected"; "not complete or full"; "disunited."[2]

Brokenness is a journey everyone must take. To be born is to be broken. We cannot enter the earth without the breaking of water. The same water that sustains us for nine months becomes the very thing we must break through. Life is filled with pregnant moments. Periods of deep darkness through which we must break through. Periods of brokenness from which we seek to be whole. The *body* experiences physical brokenness in the form of physical trauma, disease, and injury. The *mind/soul* experiences brokenness in the form of emotional trauma, stress, personal loss, and a feeling of disconnectedness from the self or others. The *spirit* experiences brokenness in the form of spiritual trauma, anger toward God, a lack of belief in God, and feeling a disconnectedness from God. When any one of these three experience brokenness, it affects the function of the other areas. Spiritual rest is where the broken places mend. Rest holds up the fragments, naked and unashamed, before God. Rest acknowledges the disconnection and draws near. Your faith and relationship with God affect your ability to feel well rested. Many of the types of rest we've been discussing affect the body and the mind; now we need to focus on restoring the spirit.

My new patient Hannah did not believe God had any role in her chronic restlessness. Her pre-appointment Google search had made it clear I believed in the connection between faith and healing. Yet still she came to me seeking my opinion on her health but insisting I do so on her terms. I've always enjoyed challenges. It's the reason I decided to practice internal medicine and why I got my bachelor's degree in biochemistry. I am fascinated by the DNA hidden within cells and the neurotransmitters at work behind every sensation. I enjoy the journey from unknown to known, from lost to found.

Legs crossed and arms folded across her abdomen, Hannah sat guarded in her seat across from me. She didn't look angry or upset. Her statement slipped out as casually as a "Yes, diabetes does run in my family." She was not confrontational. She was resolute in her lack of need for spiritual connection. I could medicate her body. I could enlighten her mind. But she made it clear I better not touch her spirit.

"Why would you leave if I mentioned Him? What do you think would happen?"

Her reply was hauntingly revealing. "Absolutely nothing."

Hannah was right. Absolutely nothing happens without relationship. Years of dead religion had left her wanting in the area of spiritual connection. She had come to see faith as a lifeless discipline with no power and no benefit.

Hannah went on to share her beliefs on spirituality. She did not believe in a Supreme Being or God of all. She believed we each carry a universal love and that this love comes from a central source. She could not tell me what that source was but stated she could tell when she was in the presence of someone who radiated this universal love. In her words, "They have a magnetic quality which draws people.

Their love is like a riptide pulling you in even when you want to fight against its power." Despite dismissing Him, she was describing Jesus.

This is where spirituality becomes confusing. It covers every religious teaching available: all gods placed in one category. Buddha sits with Jesus, the dead with the living. In this view, religion is seen as a subject to learn about and not an opportunity for a divine relationship. What if spirituality is not about learning about religion, but rather about experiencing a relationship?

Is your heart ready to explore a relationship or are you keeping it safely tucked away behind the walls of religion?

Evaluate Your Current Position

> *"A wounded spirit who can bear?"*
> PROVERBS 18:14B KJV

We all have wounds. Most of these wounds are superficial and fleeting. They leave little evidence of ever having entered our life. But some wounds cannot be so easily dismissed. These traumatic wounds penetrate into our very soul and break something deep within. The result is the pain no one talks about, the hidden pain of a broken faith, a wounded spirit, and a hemorrhaging heart. This is the pain that comes when you experience rejection by someone who is supposed to love you forever. This is the injury resulting from prolonged exposure to negative crippling words and self-defeating thoughts. This is the void felt when chronic disease becomes your daily companion. This is the gaping wound present after a child commits suicide or a natural disaster destroys your home. This is the deep ache left when death, loss, abuse, divorce, or severe physical illness enters your life. This resulting lingering pain has left many of us too wounded to trust God with our pain. We feel hopeless and helpless. It is in these moments the question arises, "Where is God when I hurt?"

The pain of our deepest wound creates a heart rift our mind cannot overcome. So in the very moments we need God the most, our pain shouts, "He cannot be trusted! Look how He's let us suffer!" The valley of our hurt penetrates into the core of who we are and changes how we view ourselves and how we view God. Pain becomes the enemy, and the goal becomes not to heal but rather to avoid hurting. But in this lies the problem. There can be no healing without pain.

Contrary to the popular saying, time does not heal all wounds. There is a process to healing, and that process is similar whether the wound is physical, emotional, or spiritual. All wounds must first be identified. The bandages covering up the issue have to be laid aside for a clear and detailed examination of the damage hiding beneath the surface. There must be a deep cleansing of the wound for healing to take place. Healthy and diseased areas can coexist but only at the risk of contaminating the thriving areas. Decay has to be removed to eliminate the competition between the diseased and healthy. Here the pain intensifies, and one must make a choice between remaining comfortably wounded and enduring the discomforts of healing. There are no viable nerve endings in dead tissue. It is without feeling. It is void of response.

It is the healthy tissue that hurts during the process of cutting away. Many never traverse this breach in healing. They resist the pain and instead seek comfort in the midst of their wounds. But pain is a vital part of the healing process. Our pain testifies that restoration back to a state of wholeness is available *if* we are willing to go through the process of healing.

Here are some signs you might be suffering from a spiritual rest deficit:

- You feel decreased satisfaction and sense of accomplishment.
- You feel helpless, hopeless, trapped, or defeated.

- You feel like life is a total waste of energy and have no motivation.
- You feel distant from God.
- You experience suicidal thoughts and depression.
- You feel numb and apathetic.

Science and Research

Despite arising from completely different poles of our understanding, faith and science do work together. Sir William Bragg was a British scientist and winner of the Nobel Prize. His opposition analogy theory offers a great visual for this. It states: "Sometimes people ask if religion and science are not opposed to one another. They are—in the sense that the thumb and finger of my hand are opposed to one another. It is an opposition by means of which anything can be grasped."[3]

Studies have demonstrated that praying and meditating affect the brain in the same way as having a conversation with a person in front of you. These studies suggest that religious activities create neurological real experiences inside of us. Experiences just as real as if God tangibly existed in a way we can touch and feel.[4] Our conversations with God imprint in our memories as if we were the ones chatting with Him in the garden.

Prayer can even make you a healthier person. Separate studies conducted at Duke, Dartmouth, and Yale Universities show that people who pray tend to get sick and become depressed less often than those who do not. In addition, it has been reported that prayer improves healing and recovery times. Prayer may seem like an insignificant part of the rest equation, but it has the potential to drastically change you.[5]

Today's Application

Each minute spent in spiritual rest exercises like meditating on Scripture, prayer, praise/worship, and journaling enlarges the capacity of your personal sanctuary. It offers rest to both the mind and the consciousness. There are many ways you can connect with God. Here are a few to consider, but don't feel confined to these suggestions. Allow room for the creative nature of God to reveal specific ways you feel most connected to Him.

Explore Relationship—God is much easier to get to know when you take religion out of the equation. As much as He would love for us all to be holy, His first request is simply to love Him. Love is not religious; love is relational. Do you remember what it was like when you were trying to get to know your lover? The long hours of talking into the night and the endless love notes all seemed as natural as humidity in Alabama. For the next seven nights, share your day with God via either written or verbal communication. No formal prayers required. No prerequisite to read a chapter in your Bible or do any other ritualistic behavior. Explore God. Just as Jesus asked His disciples, hear Him asking you, "Who do you say I am?"[6] Your quest for an answer may lead you to research the man, but don't stop there. Explore the heart of who He is, until you get to God. Relationships take time. Start building this one today.

Practice Communion—You may be like I was when I first started my journey. I wanted nothing to do with God. I didn't like Him, didn't trust Him, and didn't see a reason to ever try to understand Him or get to know Him. If that's you, start with this one courageous step: In the privacy of your secret place, lift both hands high above your head and simply profess, "I need help." Why do I want your hands above your head? Because I want you boldly reaching for what you do not understand with both hands open wide. I want you to stretch the level of your expectancy above the limits of your reason-ing. Not understanding the holy does not make you any less worthy to receive. If tears fall, it's OK. If it appears nothing has happened, that's OK. If you start shouting and cursing God at the top of your lungs, that's OK too. Healing is a journey, and part of the process is gradually removing those things that have been blocking your path to wholeness, one stumbling block at a time.

Reunite Body-Mind-Spirit—Most of us can easily see how con-necting with God can help relieve emotional and spiritual pain. But one question I'm often asked is, "How is getting in God's presence going to help my physical pain?"

Physical pain increases when you are under emotional stress and spiritual distress. Anything you can do to improve emo-tional pain will also improve how you feel physically. Take a practical step today in improving any pain you may be experi-encing by practicing entering into God's presence. First, identify any pain affecting you. Next, download the free printable heal-ing affirmation/Scripture artwork from my website's resources page at IChooseMyBestLife.com and read these as you listen to uplifting music. This should take about ten to fifteen min-utes, the same amount of time most doctors allocate for an office visit. Conclude with a simple request from your heart: "God meet with me."

Just like the patients wanting medical attention who enter my practice, if you want the help of the Healer, you must get to where He is and be still long enough to be examined. Use this approach during times when stress is exacerbating your pain and place yourself in the position for healing that flows from spiritual rest.

Chapter 8

Social Rest

Find Solace in Another

I spotted him long before he noticed me approaching. My first instinct was avoidance. I was not obligated to acknowledge him, but I was compelled to do so by the quiet confidence in his gaze. The sign he held was a simple request for help. No explanations, no excuses. He was without a home and desperately in need of warmth, shelter, and nourishment. All the cars before me kept driving by, windows up to keep the coldness out. I was still many feet from his post, yet he looked straight at me. Eye contact led to head nods and an invitation to connect. I fished a few crumpled dollars from my purse. In the passing of bills, our fingers touched, our humanity threatened to do the same. Traffic around us continued, other drivers oblivious to the exchange. He didn't even look at the money.

"Thank you, ma'am. Thank you. Would you please remember to pray for me? My name is Cody." His voice was hurried and pleading. "Remember, pray for Cody."

With the money still clenched in one hand, he extended the other to grab hold of something even more valuable—social rest. Social rest is when we find comfort in our relationships and social interactions. It is the ability to find solace in another. On this frosty day, Cody needed the rest that comes from being seen, to know someone cared enough to pray for him specifically by name. He stood with a sign asking for assistance with the necessities of life. Rest is one of those necessities, and on this day he hungrily sought to feed his need for connection.

Every life is a story, and these stories connect through your interactions at work, at home, and at play. Some parts of your story occur in lonely places. They may develop in the wake of mistakes and hardships, leaving you feeling isolated. This sense of separation has a cancerous effect on your ability to rest. Instead of being in a state of social connectedness, you remain restless around others. You feel less than and left out. The result is a level of disconnectedness that leaves you feeling despondent, depressed, and drained.

Social rest reconnects us to uplifting, rewarding relationship exchanges. We crave those moments when a friend gets our joke. We feel support when a coworker remembers our birthday. We feel loved when a spouse kisses us hello. Each interaction is seemingly small and insignificant but collectively replenishes our social rest deficit. Each helps us de-stress and boosts our overall well-being. Each fights against any feelings of isolation.

Isolation and loneliness are the two most common forms of social restlessness. This isolation can be actual or perceived. A newly widowed woman can be surrounded by family and friends and still feel deeply isolated and alone in the loss of the relationship in which she most found social rest. A first-year college student can be heavily engaged in campus activities but battle with perceived isolation because of a lack of meaningful social connections. We all need social contact to adjust our perspective on isolation and to confront our loneliness. The need for social connectedness is encrypted into your

DNA. Whether you consider yourself an introvert or an extrovert, relationships are an important part of a well-rested life. Skip too many meals and your stomach will start growling. Just as the body hungers, your soul also hungers for connection. Loneliness is the soul's plea to feed your need for social rest.

Recognize Your Risk

Relationships are where we make deposits when we are full and withdraw from when we feel empty. I aspire to be honest, authentic, and vulnerable in my interactions with others, but it's quite difficult. Relationships are hard work. The desire to represent myself well and be liked often challenges my wanting to be real. I worry that in speaking my truth I may offend someone or that they won't accept me. It's easier to shut up and just try to fit in.

Can you relate to this in your life?

We look down on fake people; however, we at times exhibit similar behavior. We become hypocritical in how we view authenticity in relationships, demanding it from others while refusing to fully participate ourselves. Social rest requires a willingness to deal with our relationship hurdles. It requires us to confront our reactions to the judgment of others, our feelings of rejection, and our fears about fitting in. In doing so, we secure relationships that give us the grace to confront our doubts, speak our truth, and be authentic.

Social rest may sound like a cry for solitude but it is actually the opposite. Social rest is about making space for those relationships that revive you. When you are with a friend you feel comfortable being around who makes you feel as if you could tell them anything, you're experiencing social rest. These social rest relationships make you feel valued and take your concerns seriously.

Social rest is how we practice the give-and-take of authentically vulnerable relationships. These relationships are very different from the majority of relationships. Most of our day-to-day interactions will be ones where we are giving our time or expertise, and gifting without the opportunity for replenishment. Most relationships take from us. It's not a bad thing. It's simply the reality of most of our interactions. Your children don't mean to be demanding when they ask what's for dinner, but they do enjoy eating more than once a day. Your spouse isn't necessarily giving you an invite to bed when he pulls you in close for a hug. As innocent as these times are, they can seem like more demands on your body and your resources.

We are also bombarded with constant superficial social interactions, especially in social media. It's not uncommon for someone to have thousands of social media friends and still feel isolated and alone. Online relationships can be a part of your social rest strategy, but too often these virtual relationships become more about striving than rest. The number of likes and shares begin to outweigh the actual communication. Social media is quickly becoming a platform for people to lash out at each other. There is no longer room for grace, harmony, and compassion. Our social reach has exceeded our social capacity. We begin spending more time minding others' business when we have plenty of business of our own to mind, not the least of which is the face-to-face relationships we ignore as we stare into our computer screens.

We are not designed to bring all these people into our home daily and interact with their every moments. We are designed to have an inner circle of relationships from which all other social interactions flow. The social overload is damaging. We have too many relationships coming at us through our screens and phones. It's easier to share our burdens remotely, void of the immediate feedback of facial expressions, voice pitch, and body language. However, in the presence of a trusted confidante, an atmosphere of rest is created. Their expressions of acceptance, understanding, and compassion become needed nourishment to conquer loneliness.

Evaluate Your Current Position

"The first cut was the hardest."

Her voice was soft and shaky there in the ER where I first encountered her, yet her statement was just a matter of fact. It was void of emotion and arose out of a place of emptiness. Long wisps of dark hair fell forward, covering her left eye but failing to hide the tears that slid down her face. These were her first words, and I had hoped the dialogue would stop there. Idle conversation was not on my agenda for the day. I had one job: stitch her back up. I was not there to counsel her. I was not obligated to go there with her, into the sacred place of her rawest emotions. If I'm completely honest, I was afraid to journey there.

I didn't want to see her fully. Looking into her eyes and seeing her truth would mean I would have to enter in as well. I didn't want to see what hid behind my walls. I had no desire to uproot pain I had mastered burying. Therefore, I looked away. I kept my eyes focused on my gloved hands. I focused on the things I could control. I could stitch together the self-inflicted cuts on her wrists. I could control her bleeding wounds. I could not control her bleeding heart. It was this bleeding that frightened me the most.

The suture needle's angle and the need for precision allowed me to maintain my emotional distance. I knew the psychiatrist would soon be by the emergency room to usher this wounded soul to a safe place for the next few days. Psychiatrists are trained to deal with this type of unraveling. I was not. I concentrated on doing the work I had been trained to do. I sutured. In silence, I reattached what had been severed. There was no numbing this pain, so I didn't even try. Not the pain in her wrist or the pain in her heart. Loneliness hurts.

The needle weaved in and out of her flesh effortlessly. As I moved around to stitch each fresh cut, I could feel her eyes staring. I don't know whether I looked like someone who would be sympathetic to her plight or if I resembled an old college friend, but whatever the reason, she wanted to confide in me. Avoiding her stare was no longer an option. Her penetrating gaze bore a hole right through my resolve. For just one second, just the amount of time it took me to switch out my suture needle and prep to suture her other wrist, I looked up into her eyes.

Large brown eyes were not looking at me; they were looking *into* me. For a moment it felt like I was the one exposed. In that brief, fleeting instant, the roles had reversed. The doctor was no longer the one inquiring of the patient, but the patient was inquiring of the doctor, "Do you sometimes feel invisible too?" If I could have looked away, it would have been easy to ignore the exchange. But I didn't. I couldn't. My soul would not let me run from this place of brutal realization. We were the same.

I had never cut my wrist, but I was the same as her. I too was medicating my loneliness. Not through cuts and self-mutilation, but through my own vices. While she resorted to a blade, my weapon of choice left little evidence of a problem. While she sought relief in watching the blood running down her arms, I sought relief in hiding behind a mask of perceived normalcy. My pain reliever was acceptable, hers not so much. We stared at each other, sisters in a battle neither wanted. Bound by a journey we'd rather not take. Confronted by decisions leading us nowhere we desired to be.

No further verbal exchange was required. I worked. She stared.

Nurses came and went. Time passed. Blood had been shed. The external bleeding had stopped. The internal bleeding continued. The isolation was real.

The tiny room the hospital assigned to resident physicians was about the size of a janitor's closet. There was just enough room for a bed and a chair. It was a room vastly too small for the magnitude of emotions I experienced that night. The bloodstained gloves were off. Wounds were cleansed. Wrists were sutured and bandaged. My patient left in the capable hands of behavioral therapists. Her bleeding had ceased. My bleeding had just begun and with it came a deep desire to be whole in my body, mind, and spirit.

Here are some signs you might be suffering from a social rest deficit:

- You feel alone in the world.
- You feel detached from family and friends.
- You are attracted to people who mistreat you or are abusive toward you.
- You find it hard to maintain close relationships or make friends.
- You isolate yourself from others.
- You prefer online relationships over face-to-face relationships.

Science and Research

Studies show that people with strong relationships live longer, cope with stress better, and are overall healthier and happier. One study of over 300,000 people found a lack of strong relationships increased the risk of premature death from all causes by 50 percent.[1] This mortality risk is greater than that caused by obesity and similar to smoking almost a pack of cigarettes a day. <u>Your social support system does</u>

more than just help you weather life's storms; it lengthens the numbers of your days.

The quality of your social connections is significantly more important than the quantity. Your social media account may reflect thousands of friends or followers. However, it's the few people who know you intimately that will have the greatest effect on you experiencing social rest. There is nothing wrong with developing a diverse network of acquaintances, but remember to nurture those closest to you. They are the ones who will be there for you through thick and thin.

Studies show an improved immune system, better cardiovascular health, and less dementia in those who regularly enjoy the companionship of close confidantes. These restful relationships can be with a spouse, a friend, or with a family member. You can even encounter moments of social rest in brief social interactions where you feel an unusual connection to another because of a shared experience. This is the rest found for many in support groups like Celebrate Recovery. These groups become a safe place for grace to flow and for the healing benefits of social rest to be manifested. There is freedom, peace, joy, hope, love, and mercy available when we find solace in another. These gifts change us and make us better people to be around.[2]

Being social with uplifting, encouraging, and life-giving people is good for you. Social rest will increase your sense of belonging and purpose. It improves your self-confidence and self-worth by defeating the lie that you are the only one who ever feels lonely or unworthy. Your socially restful relationships help you cope with the times life hurts you, such as when you must deal with a divorce, serious illness, job loss, or death of a loved one. Social rest serves to encourage you to pursue happiness through interactions with others and not simply in the accumulation of things.

Today's Application

The best part of my job is the people I meet. The hardest part of my job is the people I meet! Some relationships are far from restful. You will not be able to completely avoid people who rub you the wrong way, but you can establish some personal boundaries about whom you let into your inner circle.

Prioritize Face-to-Face Time—Technology makes it easy to send a text message, make a phone call, or email a friend. The convenience of a quick connection has cost many their ability to build strong relationships. Relationships are social investments. They grow over time as you make small deposits into them. Take a moment to identify those relationships in your life that leave you feeling rested, accepted, and at ease. Purposefully become hands-free when you are around these individuals. If your marriage is a source of social rest, turn off the TV and close your laptop when alone with your spouse. Spend time face-to-face. Looking directly into someone's eyes is a form of intimacy. Take your time in these moments. Experience the closeness of being face-to-face and use those times to find comfort in the relationships you value.

Listen and Learn—If most of your time with your closest relationships involves you talking, consider shutting up and listening. Often we feel that we are alone in our struggles and difficulties. When you give others a chance to talk, it provides an opportunity to learn. Through their transparency, you can see yourself more clearly. You become aware of the similarities in life we all experience like pain, loss, disappointment, and fear. Then in the truth of our common experiences, you can rest in knowing you are not alone. You are not the exception. You are not the one person in the universe who has messed life up so badly that it cannot be redeemed.

I was once at a spiritual counseling session when I was at a low point in my life. I wailed about my life choices when the counselor abruptly said, "So what makes you think your problems are so big and insurmountable that even God can't touch them? Believe me, no one's problems are that special." I smile now thinking about her approach; in the moment I was firing killer darts at her with my eyes.

I hate to admit it, but she was right. You are unique, and the circumstances surrounding your situation are individualized, but your heart is vulnerable just like mine. Your mind is susceptible to depression and your body yields to fatigue. All these weaknesses are not so special that they cannot be revived, restored, and renewed.

Nurture Your Need to Connect—Rest is active, restorative, and relational. Find your tribe, the people you feel naturally connected to, and you will find an endless source of social rest. Join a religious, social, or support group. Talk to like-minded people about how they live and deal with stress. Connect with a community group or champion a cause that is meaningful to you. Attend meetings or join professional associations to interact with others in your line of work who can relate to your workplace demands. Expanding your social network is often the first step in finding those people who make your world a better place. While it's important not to take on too much when you're feeling drained, connecting with others doesn't have to involve a lot of time or effort. You alone will know the right amount of social interaction needed to leave you energized and not depleted.

Chapter 9

Sensory Rest

Remove External Distractions

Perk up your imagination for a few minutes and visualize this scene with me: You are at your favorite beach. A cool ocean breeze caresses your face, tussling stray strands of hair. You inhale. The scent of your coconut sunblock hangs in the air. The early morning sun floods the area with a hazy glow and warms your skin. The fine white sand is rough against the soles of your feet, kneading the soreness away. Every crashing wave is inviting you to take a dip. You dive under the foaming peaks, enjoying the tug-of-war between your body and the currents. Your lips taste the saltiness of the sea and yearn for the tart sweetness of a mango-pineapple smoothie. On the shore awaits a hammock perched between two palm trees, ready to rock away any remaining stress.

Sounds wonderful, right? Now imagine the same scene minus your senses. Your ears deaf to the waves, your taste buds unresponsive to salt, your eyes blinded to the sun, your nose oblivious to the scents, and your sense of touch gone. Many of the best parts of living are so amazing because of the senses we associate with those experiences. We live our lives immersed in sensations. The problem is, most of us take our senses for granted. We are so attuned to constant sensory input, we've learned to block out much of it. We have adapted to our noisy, artificially lit world with a keen ability to ignore what we don't want to deal with.

Our overly busy and overly stimulating society has created the perfect environment for sensory overload, each technology advancement chipping away at the sanctity of our five senses. When I started practicing medicine over eighteen years ago, the majority of my time was spent looking into the eyes of my patients. Now I find myself spending more and more hours of my day staring at electronic health records on a computer screen. Diabetes, hypertension, and obesity statistics climb yearly as our taste buds crave saltier, creamier, and sweeter foods in order to feel satisfied. The ability to enjoy simplicity has been anesthetized and with it the loss of our ability to experience sensory rest.

Sensory rest involves denying one or more of your senses the experience of the physical world for short periods. Total sensory deprivation is an impossible goal. It would mean no sounds, no vision, no smells, no tastes, and no feeling including the touch of the clothes on your skin. You use at least one of your five senses every moment of every day. Your senses work together to notify your brain of what is going on around you. They help keep you safe by warning you of danger.

Every day your nervous system is under constant stimulation. Background music plays in offices, in elevators, and while your phone call is placed on hold. Television, computers, iPads, and smartphones add their artificial glow to your environment. The popcorn burning in the break room mingles with the latest perfume and fragrant hand lotion to overwhelm your nasal passages. Our bodies crave a reprieve. Periodic times of selective sensory deprivation deliberately remove external distractions and stimuli from your senses in order to reenergize them.

Recognize Your Risk

I love movies, with the smells of buttery popcorn and ear-tickling sur-round sound. With two preteen boys, our family movie night usually involves the latest flicks with either the most action or the most fight-ing, or if they are lucky a movie with lots of action *and* fighting. The last movie we watched had me on the edge of my seat, and I was in dire need of a bathroom visit when it concluded. Public bathrooms are cha-otic. Wall-to-wall people dancing around praying they don't have an accident before a stall becomes available. My position in line was right in front of the sink. In the few minutes I stood there, I experienced sen-sory overload. Automatic toilets flushed, touch-free hand dryers roared at an ear-numbing volume, fluorescent overhead lights shone bright, the chemical smell of strawberries (or what I think was supposed to be some type of berry) polluted the windowless air, a baby lay screaming on the changing table, a smelly used diaper by his side, and the sound of numerous conversations all hit my senses at once. After two hours of smelling high-fat treats and listening to crashing metal and yelling from the speakers, my five senses were done for the night.

There was a time when life was slower, and we could enjoy the sounds and smells of living. Now life zooms by in a noisy blur, filled with images, sounds, and smells everywhere we turn. Our excessive exposure to non-stop sensory information has left many of us exhausted. We accept the health benefits of avoiding junk food, but we rarely consider the effects of the junky cluttered sensory impressions we receive from our choices of entertainment or living environment. When your senses are receiv-ing input from fast-moving video games, frantic TV scene changes, and strobe lights, they become strained from the relentless release of informa-tion. Short bursts of these activities can be fun and should be enjoyed. But if you notice yourself becoming anxious or irritable after a weekend movie marathon, or if your teen becomes more agitated after hours of playing videos games, sensory overload may be the cause of these behavioral changes. When you overload the senses, you overload the mind, and your body and emotions will respond adversely. Signs of a restless overstimulated body include racing thoughts, anger, palpitations, anxiety, disturbing dreams, and trouble falling to sleep.

You may work in a situation with just as many sensory inputs. Sensory stimuli can be a combination of sounds, smells, colors, lights, or persistent motion. Each has the potential to deplete your senses and leave you at risk for sensory overload. When your brain is overcome with too much sensory input, it can become incapable of effectively processing the information. This overload of sensations stresses the body and the mind.

The type of work you do can predispose you to different kinds of sensory overload. Your hearing can be overstimulated if you work around loud noises, large groups where multiple conversations are going on at once, constant background noise/music, loud alarms, children's cries or yells, or loud appliances, machinery, or tools. Your vision can experience overload from bright lights, excessive blue light exposure from electronics, constantly changing scenes on television, a work environment with lots of movement, or cluttered environments with very little white space for the eyes to rest. Your sense of smell is at risk when you are often surrounded by numerous people wearing perfume, areas with chemical cleaning products, environments with aromatic personal care fragrances, smoke, excessive pollution, or strong food aromas. Your taste buds may be experiencing signs of exhaustion if you find yourself craving sugar, salt, fatty foods, spicy foods, and processed foods because you no longer think fruits, vegetables, and whole foods taste good. Your sense of touch can become overstimulated if your day-to-day activities require you to touch or be touched by others, and if your hands are constantly at work typing on a keyboard, picking up children, cleaning dishes, folding laundry, or doing any other type of manual labor. Our bodies deserve a break from the onslaught of activity and sensation.

Evaluate Your Current Position

Her kids devoured the small space of my exam room like it was the indoor playground at their favorite fast-food chain. The oldest was full of energy. He climbed onto my stool and twirled around in a circle. Around and around he went, oblivious to the two adults in the room. The middle child was fascinated by my otoscope hanging on the wall. He climbed onto the closest chair in an attempt reach it. Thankfully, he was a wee bit too short to succeed. In another two years, my equipment would be in serious jeopardy. Her youngest lay across her lap. She moved her daughter slightly during my exam to make room for my inquiring stethoscope. Despite the life radiating from the three small bodies surrounding her, this mommy looked worn-out.

"I need a break," she confided.

I asked her about the last time she got away to do something fun, something just for her. Her reply opened my eyes to my limited definition of what it means to take a break.

"When I say that I need a break, I'm not talking about a vacation or a special getaway. I'm not trying to get out of doing my responsibilities or bail out on my obligations. I enjoy being a stay-at-home mom. I love my kids. I love my life. I just need time in my day to feel like I come first. I spend most of every day giving away my love and energy to others. I need to learn how to spend a little of that love and energy on myself. I need a break, so I don't break."

We all need a break, a time to rediscover life in small tangible ways and to rediscover ourselves apart from the people we serve, the roles we play, the titles we carry, and the goals yet fulfilled. Similarly, our senses need a break. For most of us, the only time we get to process the deluge of information our senses receive during our day is when we sleep. This is an ineffective way to preserve and optimize the function of our senses. When our senses continue receiving incoming information without a break, the nervous system becomes too congested to process the information appropriately. The result is a decline in happiness, stifled creativity, mental restlessness, and blunted performance. Ultimately your overall health suffers because of inadequate sensory rest.

Here are some signs you might be suffering from a sensory rest deficit:

- You have a sensitivity or an adverse reaction to loud sounds.
- You experience blurry vision and/or eye pressure, fatigue, or strain.
- You believe natural foods don't have any flavor and crave processed foods.
- You dislike being hugged or touched by others.
- You are desensitized to aromas others seem to smell easily.
- You are unable to enjoy periodic sensory-rich experiences like concerts or fireworks.

Science and Research

Studies show that 58 percent of adults experience eye strain from overexposure to computers. These numbers are likely to be much higher in the future as schools and colleges use more digital resources. Computer vision syndrome can lead to headaches, blurry vision, dry eye, and neck and shoulder pain. The American Optometric Association (AOA) suggests limiting these effects by following the 20-20-20 rule. Take a 20-second break every 20 minutes and view something at least 20 feet away. These 20-second breaks force you to use counteracting eye muscles, which decreases eye fatigue and strain. Other things you can do to avoid eye strain include lowering the brightness of your monitor—research shows that when you lower the brightness, the reduction in your ability to focus drops by half and you feel less fatigued.[1]

Noise-related hearing loss is another common workplace health issue. The Centers for Disease Control reports over four million workers go to work each day in damaging noise.[2] If you have difficulty hearing what others say at your job or have to shout to be understood when standing only a few feet away, noise levels in your work environment may be at a hazardous range. This risk is present regardless of the noise or the source. There are some screaming toddlers who can pierce your eardrums as effectively as the shrill hum of loud machinery. Early identification and safety measures like hearing protection and noise reduction practices could save you from future hearing loss.

Today's Application

Unplug—Too much external stimulation clogs up your life and slows down the flow of rest in your body. The more plugged in and connected you are, the more restless you will feel. Try setting a time each day when you completely disconnect from technology. Yes, zero electronics—no TV, no cell phone, no computer. Just you unplugged from the world and plugged into rest. The world won't stop if you miss a Facebook post and your life will not suffer from ignoring a few texts or tweets. The most stressed-out people in my practice are those most responsive to their technology. You don't have to be a slave to your equipment. Avoid automatically responding every time you get a notice that you have a message. Stop obeying your electronic taskmasters. They were created to work for you, not to lord over you. Hold firm to your resolve to honor that twenty minutes or one hour you set aside to unplug. Make this time sacred. You can use this time in conjunction with other restful activities like stretching, praying, meditating, or simply just being still.

Test Your Sensory Response—Not all sensory input is created equal. Some sounds, smells, tastes, or textures cause you to feel more relaxed and peaceful. Experiment with how different types of sensory input affect you. For example, if your day is void of music, you may find it restful to immerse yourself in it. In health care, I spend a large portion of my day categorizing sundries of smells, from body waste to antiseptics. Fresh air is not always an option, but citrus aromatherapy hand creams create moments of freshness until I can enjoy the real thing. Our sense of touch is often underwhelmed by our day. Determine fabrics that promote calmness in you. Many women who have trouble sleeping at night go to bed in rough terry yoga pants and a T-shirt. Test your body's response to sleeping in softer fabrics like silk. Practice different sensory inputs and monitor how they make you feel. Taste, see, feel, smell, and listen with the liberty to add or subtract from the sensory inputs in your life.

Identify and Target—Think of just one sensory stressor you often encounter during your day, such as background music in your workplace, blue light from electronic screens, or fragrant perfumes on your coworkers. Target that particular sensory stressor and look for restful alternatives to undo the effect of that specific constant stimulation. Alleviate constant noise with periods of silence. Rest your vision with periods of darkness. Restore your nasal passages with periods of fresh air. Wash your palate with pure water. Reinvigorate the sensitivity of your senses. After a few weeks, target a second sensory stressor and continue the process until you are comfortable downgrading your sensory input as part of your well-rested life.

Chapter 10

Creative Rest

Soak in Beauty and Light

My friend Eva and I can stand atop a cliff overlooking a waterfall pooling into an aqua-blue oasis beneath us and have completely different experiences. I will lean over the railing and marvel at the power of the water and thrill at the fine spray of mist it leaves on my face. Eva, on the other hand, will be ten feet away, paintbrush in hand, capturing it all. The same spot that's creating a peaceful memory in my spirit is opening up art in my friend. Art is not work for Eva; art is how she rests in God. His creation is her muse. Immersion in serenity unlocks her creative juices.

Eva isn't the only one who responds to beauty. In my years of counseling patients, I've noticed a connection between those who are happy, productive, and living fully. They all regularly participate in what I call creative rest. It is the rest one finds when immersed in creative beauty. I sometimes affectionately refer to it as beauty rest. This creative rest is why many feel peaceful when in the mountains or at the beach, or when observing great paintings or listening to classical music. Whether natural or man-made, all beauty is a creative work. Our soul yearns to be awed and captivated. When we're deprived of these opportunities, depression and apathy arise within us. Creative rest revives our failing hearts. Life becomes more enjoyable when we soak in beauty and light.

In the beginning, God created the heavens and the earth. He called light into being and separated it from the darkness. He separated the sky from the seas. He illuminated the day with the sun and sprinkled the night with stars. He created the sea and filled it with creatures. He fashioned and formed every living thing from ants to lions to humans. And then, He rested from all His work. He blessed the seventh day and made it holy.[1] God contemplated His own work, saw that it was good, and then He did something unexpected. God rested. Not only did He introduce the concept of rest, He intentionally designed and practiced it. He was committed to setting a foundation for sacred rest from the very beginning of time. He knew rest mattered, so He rested from the work of creation. He did not take a vacation or a temporary leave of absence. He remained God in the rest. He continued to sustain all that He had created while He rested. He paused to enjoy the beauty and light before Him.

In creation, God established a pattern of work and rest for us to follow—a divine example of the benefits of creative rest and how it brings out an appreciation of the good. In a world of so much devastation, evil, and contention, it can be difficult finding the good in life. I've often turned on the TV or my laptop in a pleasant mood, only to have it crushed with news of shootings, protests, pestilence, and wars. How much can our spirits bear? How long can we juggle the heaviness before it comes crashing down upon us? We need periods of creative rest to rejoice in and contemplate God's work. We need His example to show us what creative rest looks like.

God is not static, repetitive, or common, and neither is His rest. The rest of God is best understood by visiting the garden once again.

In these first moments of God and man, we can better understand the concept of creative rest.

The rest of God sets you free to actively enjoy your life. It fulfills your needs without diminishing your resources. It awakens you to the possibilities available. Creative rest uses all God has created around us to create something inside of us. What is created is as unique as each individual.

Restlessness entered the human experience when we got our first bite from the tree of the knowledge of good and evil. With that first taste came our struggle with rest. We wrestle against the evil and the afflictions by which this present life is marred.[2] We are weary from the evil we see, and it leaves us searching for the good in the world.

Recognize Your Risk

A misconception of creative rest is that it is rest solely for creative people or that it is rest that will result in a work of creativity like art, poetry, or music. Creative rest is not about putting a demand on your creative ability; that's not rest, that's work. It is the opposite. It's allowing white space in your life and giving room for your creativity to show up. Creative rest lets you focus on your basic need for wonder. You can enjoy fulfilling that basic need in ways that don't put any pressure on your being creative. Yes, creativity may bloom from the seeds planted, but creativity is not the objective, only rest.

If your day-to-day requires you to think outside the box, you will be prone to be deficient in creative rest. Authors get writer's block. Musicians lose their groove. Moms lose their zest for life. Husbands forget the awe of loving well. Jobs with high demands on your creativity will require greater periods of creative rest to rejuvenate and liberate your creative juices.

pg .101

Your habitual environment can become ineffective in being conducive to creative rest. I find I am best able to experience creative rest when I am near bodies of water, large or small. Oceans, lakes, ponds, or fish tanks will work to stir up something inside me. My friend Donna is also a water lover. She is empowered by the water, so much so that she uprooted her family a few years ago and moved into her dream home by the beach. I loved our video catch-up time because of the sounds of beach life captured. A few years after her move, I noticed Donna started talking more about traveling to different parts of the world. Each place she named was beach-less. Once her beloved beach became her habitual environment, Donna needed a new creative rest spot. On a missionary trip to Colombia, she found her muse in the creative beauty of the Andes Mountains.

If you live in an urban area void of nature, look for local parks and nature trails. The change in scenery will cause your mind and spirit to recalibrate the new input of its surroundings. It's like rebooting your computer. We all need an occasional reboot. If you live in the flat plains of the Midwest, an occasional getaway to the mountains or the beach may be just what you need to replenish waning enthusiasm for life. The amazing thing about creative rest is its ability to leave lasting impressions on us. Do you recall the first time you saw a breathtaking sight, like the Grand Canyon, the beach, the Rockies, Niagara Falls, or the Northern Lights? These moments of creative rest are hard to forget. We can't experience these times daily, but we can seek out daily creative rest in small wonders like the sound of a baby's laugh, the colors of a butterfly's wings, the appearance of a rainbow, the fragrance of a blooming flower, or the fluttering in your soul when your love looks into your eyes. It's these small miracles of creation that have the greatest power to restore joy to our lives.

big

Small

Evaluate Your Current Position

Have you lost appreciation for the simple beauty of creation?

I've trampled over many petals on my way to the life I thought I wanted. I pushed past the smiles of people I love. I ran hard in the direction of my goals. It was a time of great productivity but lacked satisfaction. I crave sustainable levels of satisfaction in my life. Not to say my life must always be in a season of good. No life is without ups and down. But it is possible to be satisfied in your innermost being, satiated on the journey of living.

Life itself is captured in the concept of creative rest. People were the final creation before God's complete approval of rest. We are not made for rest; rest was made for us. Rest is God's gift back to His people. His presence is how He connects us to His rest. It is part invitation and part prescription.[3] We are invited to see Him in creation, come when we are weary, and draw near to rest our soul. While the promise of rest in His presence remains continually available, I at times find myself fighting to enter in. Let's just be honest, rest ranks right up there with exercise. We all know it's good for us. Knowledge alone is not enough. Dysfunction is often the key motivator for people to honor themselves with adequate rest.

Rest for a moment, and listen to the still small voice of truth instructing you to escape the cycle of busy. Rest is available, even now in the midst of the deadlines due, the people vying for your attention, the bills you hope you can pay this month, and the ambitions you strive to fulfill. As you soak in the rays of the rising sun, breathe the fresh air of the summer rain, or heed the canary's call to sing a new song, may your toil be suspended long enough to remind you of the rest readily available to you. We may not all be able to afford a $200 hour-long hot stone massage, but we can all enjoy creative rest. It is no respecter of persons. It is there for the taking daily. You are the only obstacle you will have to overcome.

Here are some signs you might be suffering from a creative rest deficit:

- You always focus on the needs of others and don't consider your needs a priority.
- You talk yourself out of self-care as if you don't deserve being cared for.
- You feel you are being selfish whenever you consider doing something for yourself.
- You do self-destructive things or make choices that sabotage your happiness.
- You rarely feel your work is of value or that others appreciate your contributions.
- You find it difficult to enjoy things in nature or in their natural state.

Science and Research

Years ago when I first started looking into medical reasons for the complaints of fatigue my female patients had, I started looking into vitamin deficiencies as a cause. Most wanted me to give them the infamous B12 shot their friends were raving about that gave them instant energy. I'm not one to jump on most nutritional bandwagons without a good dose of supporting research. I started checking the vitamin levels of these ladies and found B12 deficiency to be quite uncommon. However, I found a disproportionate number of women with severe vitamin D deficiency. A perplexing situation, since vitamin D is naturally made by the body when it's exposed to the sun. Most of these women had very fair complexions and had been warned by doctors, media, and their makeup suppliers to avoid the sun for fear of skin damage and the potential for skin cancer. As with many things in medicine, we went to an unhealthy extreme and now need to recant our statements. The body needs vitamin D. It is essential for healthy bones, skin, and mental well-being. Being D deficient may increase the risk of many chronic diseases, such as osteoporosis and heart disease, as well as infectious diseases, such as the seasonal flu, and mental illnesses like depression. I've found some of my most depressed patients drastically improve with daily limited sun exposure. Most medical professionals now advocate ten to fifteen minutes of unprotected sun exposure for those with no known history of skin disease or cancer, then play it safe by using sunscreen.[4]

Studies have also shown our brains are most at rest in natural environments like the beach. Brain imaging studies in one report showed a lot less brain activity when participants looked at pictures of the sea compared to when they viewed images of green spaces, suggesting "it's possibly less stressful and more familiar to the core of human beings."[5] The research in this area is still ongoing as scientists investigate the reasons humans love water and the health benefits of being in these natural environments.

Today's Application

- **Build Sabbaticals into Your Life**—Take a look at your calendar for the next few weeks. Block out a specific time for sabbatical. It can be thirty minutes, a few hours, a weekend, or an entire week. The duration will depend on your current situation. Decide how you want to spend your time. Loosely plan how your days will look. A lack of a plan for your sabbatical time often results in idleness and pointless ceasing. Instead of aimlessly doing nothing, purposely cease depleting activities and engage in those that rejuvenate you. You want your periods of cessation to reap a harvest of restfulness. Consider outdoor activities you seldom have time to enjoy. Visit locations you'd like to explore. Grab your backpack, a few bottles of water, fruits, nuts, a notepad, and a camera for the road. Allow room in your calendar to be wooed by creation. Hike to a hidden water-fall. Peek through the window of a newborn nursery. Sit on the steps of your office building watching the antics of a street-savvy pigeon. You are the judge and jury of your sabbatical time. Stop feeling condemned when your creative rest needs do not line up with conventional sabbatical activities. As you build sabbaticals into your life, you will learn to daily slip in and out of periods of restfulness in the midst of great productivity.

Practice Flow-Break Rhythm—Just as the sun and the moon have a natural rhythm, our bodies and minds have a natural rhythm for optimal performance. For most, those rhythms are in ninety-minute to two-hour increments.[6] Practice flowing in your daily activities in these time blocks followed by twenty minutes of a scheduled rest break. Get in the habit of flow-break-repeat. If you are habitually attached to your phone, make it work for you. Set a timer to chime every one and a half to two hours. Make it a sound you don't typically hear, preferably something pleasant to the ears. Let that sound become your per-sonal invitation to rest. What activity do you need to get done today that would normally take you hours to complete? Get busy with the work, but don't neglect the times of rest. Ready, set, flow!

Work with Your Body Clock—The circadian rhythm is a natu-ral cycle that tells our bodies when to wake up, when to go to sleep, and when's the best time for every activity on your to-do list. It's our body's internal clock keeping time with the rhythm of healthy living. It is affected by the amount of sunlight we are exposed to, the temperature of the room we sleep in, and even the types of food we consume. If your circadian rhythm is disrupted, it will adversely affect your sleep, rest, and performance. Work with your body's clock by doing activities during the time of best opportunity. Studies show it's best to do high brain function activities before noon when your mental capacity is naturally at its peak. The time between one and four p.m. is when studies show we are more likely to become distracted. Use this time frame to do activities that require less of your attention. Creativity tends to peak in the evening hours. Adjust your schedule one day this week to incorporate your must-do activities during the times your body is wired to respond optimally. Work with your body's internal clock and you will find yourself being more productive with less effort.[7]

Chapter 11

Give It a Rest

The Bible at times reads like a collection of remote stories, far removed from my day-to-day life. It doesn't speak to my current difficulties, my pains, my troubles, but to a people I do not know, in a culture untainted by the havoc overwhelming my life.

And then there are those days when the heart of God speaks to me through the pages. In these moments, the Bible becomes a part of me. My heart, my soul, and my spirit recognize the holiness of a word in season, and those words bring life, truth, and understanding. My mind fights truth. It wars against accepting truth because my mind wants to hold on to what it can easily understand. The sacred is unexplainable. It bears witness with our soul without the need for interpretation. For years I shunned its advances and excused myself from living the life I desired. My excuses were my safety, every excuse an anchor in a river of unrelenting truth. Every excuse rejecting the possibility of a better way. Rest is its own excuse and warrants no further explanation. Lovely is a life anchored in rest.

Let's tackle those excuses that pull us away from rest. I've heard from men and women on the heart-pounding end of my stethoscope. Each explains why their lives are too busy to take a break. Kids need to be chauffeured to and from practices. Aging parents need to be carried to and from doctors' appointments. Employees live paycheck to paycheck, no margin for vacation or time off. Workers look forward to overtime as a means to the excess they desire. Time at work is exchanged for family time, leading to deeper dysfunction. Moms and dads exchange opportunities to listen to growing children with moments to give voice to their parental frustration with their teen's progress. Time is spent daily, heavy on the heartache and light on happiness. This is life, but this is not living. Life can be overwhelming, and it's going to keep coming at you. It doesn't cease. You have to choose to slow it down. You have to decide to turn your energy back toward *rest*oration (or to keep it simple, back toward rest).

So what are these excuses really about? Excuses are invented reasons we create to defend our behavior. It's how we rationalize our neglect and how we avoid taking responsibility for our choices. It allows us to place blame on God and anyone else around so that we don't have to be accountable for our decisions. With excuses, we place external blame for internal problems and stay in a cycle of unproductivity.

We make these excuses for various reasons, but the most prevalent is fear. We fear change. We fear uncertainty. We fear responsibility. We fear failure, and many even fear success. If you want to eliminate these excuses, you have to first do the heart work of untangling any remnants of fear present. Fear wants to stop you, to keep you out of the place of rest you desire. It wants to keep you in a place of lack—a lack of understanding and a lack of perspective. We perish when we lack knowledge.[1]

The burned-out life you're living is all the proof you need that your excuses have lasting consequences. Not only will they prevent you from living a life you enjoy, but they also hold you back from reaching your full potential and from recognizing the numerous opportunities before you, opportunities to choose well—to choose truth over lies, faith over fear, peace over conflict, forgiveness over bitterness, and rest over struggle.

Your excuses can construct imaginary mental walls—mental blocks that reinforce bad judgment and self-limiting beliefs. These life-draining consequences can never lead to a fulfilling life. They paralyze you and prevent you from moving forward. You must first be truthful with yourself and admit why you're making excuses if you want to break free from their gravitational pull on your life.

If you are ready to give those excuses a rest, begin by asking yourself these questions. What excuses do I make? Why am I making these excuses? What are these excuses preventing me from experiencing? How are these excuses limiting my ability to get what I want? Why am I settling for a life of excuses?

Here are the top five excuses I hear:

"There's not enough time already to do everything I want to do, so how am I going to find time for rest?"

"I don't know how to do these different types of rest described. It's too complicated."

"I can't change overnight."

"This won't work."

"I need time to plan how I'm going to incorporate rest in my life."

Let's plan to unplan a few things in your day. What would happen if you paused for a moment, shut your eyes, tightened and released your neck muscles, listened to the sound of nothing, and let your mind quiet down? The world would not end nor would everything in your life come into alignment. Instead, in that moment, you would restore part of the energy pouring out of you, and you would leave that moment better than how you entered it.

If these pauses were part of your daily bread, part of your daily inhalation of life, you would spend more of your day enjoying the moments in between. This is the next step in your opportunity to focus on the solutions rather than the excuses. An opportunity to begin putting your energy into changes that can immediately transform your perspective and build up your reserves.

What are your excuses? What are you going to do with this invitation to do the simple, to lay the heavy down, to find the time to be restored, to recover what's been lost, and to revive your happiness?

Please Excuse My Dust, Life in Progress

It's no coincidence I named my youngest son Isaiah. It was in the book of Isaiah that I started hearing the heart of God on the topic of rest. The truth of this Scripture lay upon my shoulders like a cashmere shawl on a crisp fall day. Its warmth is far-reaching and satisfying. Its truth came at a time when I had no excuses left. I was at my lowest point, exhausted and extinguishing. In Isaiah 30:12–15, God is talking to the people about the many promises He has told them to expect in their lives. Great promises they have yet to see. The delays have made them skeptical of His faithfulness. The hard times have made them question His love. He explains to them it is not by His choice they have not seen the promises fulfilled; it is by their choices.

His reply as I interpreted it: "You hate this word I'm telling you. You would rather trust in a system that has been driving you into the ground and rely on that system more than you would like to rely on My way of doing things. That's why you're in the situation you're in now. You mistrust truth, and that mistrust is a high wall you are afraid to traverse. But traverse it you must, because staying put will lead to a collapse, a breaking that will come suddenly. It will be like a vessel ruthlessly smashed to the ground, leaving in its wake unrecognizable fragments. All that will be left are the shards of the promise. Listen now to the solution. In returning and resting you shall be saved, in quietness and trust shall be your strength. But you are unwilling. You are unwilling to do the simple. You resist doing what should come naturally. You would rather do that which is hard. You would rather struggle than rest. You would rather work under a sense of obligation than learn how to surrender to peace. You would rather fight for every blessing rather than trust goodness is following you. You would rather see it before you believe it. You are afraid of rest."

If you search for this Scripture, you will find I have not quoted it word for word. A quote would not have had the power to ignite the fire of my smoldering life. On this particular day these words came alive, and as I read the simple Scripture, it became a living message. It confronted my excuses and called me out from my hiding place. It dared me to stay put and warned me about the destruction to come if I failed to respond. It was a clarion call shouting from the high places in my heart, "Return and rest!"

He was right; I was afraid of rest. I had every right to be afraid of rest. Rest is a daunting proposition when you've worked for everything you have. Privilege did not come with my birth package. A better life came with a hefty cost, the most valuable of which was my soul. I no longer found this price acceptable in my life. It is not acceptable for your life either.

It's time to give it a rest. It's time to stop with the excuses and the reasons we have to maintain the status quo. It's time to lay aside the notion of endless work being the end to the means. It's time to stop trying to fulfill every promise by our blood, sweat, and tears. It's time to go back to the beginning when rest was required, when rest was sacred. When quietness was not a weakness and trust was not something to fear. Where we saw them for what they truly are, needed ingredients in a life worth living. Return to rest, quietness, and trust as a deer returns to a stream. Return to the source of your strength, and in doing so, you will be saved. Rest is salvation. It pulls you back from the edge and replenishes the emptiness of daily pouring out into your days.

Rest is a taste of heaven. This is what we've been missing. This is what we've been seeking. In our haste for quick relief, we have sought to run in the direction of more activity and turned to everything except rest. We run from the rest we desperately need toward a life desperate for a release. Now I ask, what are you running from and to?

A few months before my fortieth birthday I decided I wanted to run my first half marathon. It would have been a great idea, but I had never run in my life and was not in the best shape. Let's just say my thighs and hips were not running material. This, however, did not stop my ambitious self from signing up for a February race. I would have five months to whip my body into shape. Goals are my friends. Give me a clear goal, and I'll get it done. Give me something abstract like rest, and I'm flailing in the wind. Thirteen-point-one miles was a concrete goal. Run, walk, crawl, or roll, one way or another I'd be crossing the finish line.

I set out one cold morning toward the end of my training to do a ten-mile run. It was blistering cold in the thirties with blasts of high winds. It was so cold I didn't anticipate being drenched in sweat when I finished and returned to my car. Did you know sweat can freeze? I had no clue. These are the things they don't teach you in medical school. They also don't tell you that when training for a half marathon your legs will feel like jelly at the end of your runs. I flopped into my car, and the second my body hit the seat a poof of dust arose. I jumped out of the car twice as fast as I had gotten in it. Fear can make a body move. I inspected the seat and found nothing. By now I was beyond cold and ready to be home in a hot shower. I lugged my achy body back into the car, and again a faint cloud of dust arose the moment I was in the seat. That's when it hit me. I pulled off the light jogging jacket I had on and found a fine layer of white powder on my arms. The salt from my sweat had dried to leave behind a powdery residue. Life is a lot like training for a run. Everyone's responsible for their race. What you put in is what you get out. If you want a better pace, you have to invest in building up your foundation. Running is most effective when combined with appropriate periods of rest and recovery. You'll find when you slow down the things you've been looking for can finally catch up with you. And, sometimes, you need a T-shirt that reads, "Please excuse my dust, life in progress."

Rest reveals things about ourselves, and that process can be messy. You may find something you didn't expect. You may find fears you never knew you had but also the energy to confront those fears. Rest frees you to open yourself to a life that scares you. This is the secret to a life well lived. In resting, you find freedom to live the life you desire. In resting, you receive the strength to do, be, and overcome everything you currently feel powerless to confront. In resting, you open the door to more power than you've ever known.

Can I just be blunt? Many of us run from rest because it seems like giving up. Rest looks a lot like waiting, and resting feels like a lack of progress. That's the lie this life wants you to believe. It's only a lie. Lies are just twisted truths awaiting a revelation. A well-rested life requires a delicate balance between pruning and growth. Some things must be cut away to make room for what's to come. Rest is not always pleasant, but it ensures that the activities, the relationships, and the situations that deplete you will not continue to be depleting.

The journey is not always comfortable. It doesn't always feel right in the moment. I don't want you to expect to see the heavens open and angels descend every time you set aside time to rest. Yes, there will be some miraculous moment where all things come together, and you feel an instant tangible change. But there will also be times when your level of depletion will require you to diligently seek the rest you need until your change comes.

Chapter 12

Finding a Sweet
Place to Land

Some women walk, she sauntered. Her entrance into the room was a swirl of confidence and assurance. Many joined me in my blatant gawking at this unknown mama daring to enter our Moms in Prayer meeting like a queen on display. Silence is a gracious space, but the hush in the conversations contained little grace. We, the mamas with the facial stress lines and extra pounds from emotional eating, were in no mood to extend grace. We were too tired to attempt such heavy lifting. So we acted like we didn't see her, like we didn't notice her invading our comfort zone. Contentment has a quality that refuses to be ignored. In the presence of someone at home in their own life, you can feel the welcome mat of relationship rolled out to usher you in. Curiosity compelled me to hover near. When you're faced with the option to envy or encounter, always encounter.

Prayers went up for our little ones, yet my heart was not in a position to release petitions to heaven. I was in a posture of prayer, head bowed and eyes closed, but my spirit had checked out of the exchange. I was jealous. I knew nothing about Unknown Mama. I had no information about her life, her socioeconomic status, or her career path.

Heck, I didn't even know who her kids were. I was envious of her comfort in her own skin. Nowhere in my discerning had I come to understand the depths of longing available when one sees what is possible. On this day watching Unknown Mama exuding self-mastery and happiness taunted me to dare to believe for more. The aroma of her contentment spoke to the unbridled power of the life she lived.

Call it a character trait of my inquisitive nature, but some part of me always questions the obvious. I wasn't convinced her happiness was genuine. The surface reflection of a life is not always a true reflection of the heart. As a doctor, I get to see people unmasked. Not the façade of who they hope to be, but the reality of who they are in this moment. I see them naked. Naked of lies. Where "I'm fine" has no business and truth becomes its own medicine. The truth of who they are, the truth of their physical health, their emotional health, and even their spiritual health. The truth of where they live.

I resolved to become a sister with the one whom I envied. My envy dared me to go deeper into her life to see whether her truth was really true. I hungered to learn what lay beneath the surface of her resolve. What secrets would lead to a life of peace, joy, and happiness? The realization of what she revealed to me was so much deeper than anything I ever expected. I wanted a quick-fix option for the lifelong changes I needed. Unknown Mama showed me a slowed-down approach to an accelerated life.

It's hard to be friends with someone who isn't friendly. I'd love to say I was oozing good feelings toward Unknown Mama. I was not. Still, through some act of fate, she sat by me. Our clasped hands in the prayer circle formed a physical bond long before our hearts intertwined. I was ready to disclaim her truth. I was ready to confront her happiness to see what her real life was like. Her eyes held no beguilement. I sensed her presence wasn't lying. She was who she was without apology. And so our lives merged from that day forward. I stepped into her life and she into mine. My family ate dinner with her family. My kids played with her kids. I held her baby, and she held mine. I invaded the oasis of her life like a woman trapped in the desert too long.

One weekend we decided to plan a getaway to a women's conference. Just the two of us, away from the husbands, away from the kids. A moment to break free from our familiar settings to taste responsibility freedom. The babies were left with the daddies as we carved out time to ourselves for a weekend of laughter, an opportunity to be heart-sisters as we shared the desires of our hearts and the longings of our passions. We met up at the hotel in separate cars, just in case life threw a curveball with a sick child or any other home emergency. The massive hallway of lights danced like Fourth of July sparklers, cheering us on as we found our room. We were ready for the weekend celebration to begin.

The lineup of speakers for the weekend included women with a reputation for sharing life honestly and openly. The opening session was everything we anticipated. It was a great time of laughter and a great time of community with like-minded women. Late that night we sat in our parallel double beds chatting about the day and then the inevitable happened. Silence. The quiet settled in the room like a reverential hush and this time grace followed. Unknown Mama was no longer unknown. I did not see her through eyes of rivalry but eyes of comradery. Now she was someone whose public life had shown itself to be a reflection of her secret life.

Hidden in Plain Sight

"Are you happy?"

Happy. Some words need clarification. Happiness or, more accurately, the pursuit of it, has been my lifelong ambition. It is the moving target I daily aim for but often miss. It has stayed just beyond my grasp but close enough to remind me of its possibility.

"Sure, I guess I'm as happy as the next girl," I replied.

My friend's next words carved a place in my soul, and through that opening, hope poured in as doubt seeped out. "I was afraid of that. What if the next girl isn't happy? Stop looking at her as the finish line."

Sometimes the lights come on all of a sudden. At other times you have to feel around in the dark to find the switch. I had just been blinded by the glare of her affront.

"You deserve to be happy, but you have to be willing to mine happiness for yourself. You have to go deep into the darkness, past your fears and insecurities, before you can begin to get a glimpse of it. I'm most happy when I'm in the world but not of the world. When my why is not wrapped up in material things but in things of eternal worth. I'm most happy when my life has room to expand, and I have the liberty to expand with it. The life you seek you already have available to you; you just haven't given yourself space to explore it. Your choices either create space or destroy it. Find the place your soul longs to rest and dwell there. There you will find the secret to living well."

Needless to say, I didn't sleep much that night. She was like a canary freed from her cage glancing back to sing a song of encouragement for those still bound. I was bound by family pressures, work stressors, and daily fatigue, but my captivity was losing its power to contain me. Our girls' weekend ended the following evening, but the life lessons continued.

To Bee or Not to Bee

I love biology, and thankfully both of my sons are just as fascinated with creation. So when one of my boys came home curious about the inner lives of honeybees, I was more than happy to be his study buddy. It's amazing how something small and insignificant can provide intense sweetness and vital nourishment. We typed "bees" into Google search and waded through some sites full of great facts. Our perseverance led us to an interesting video on the life cycle of bees and the inner workings of the hive. We learned that worker bees are all female, the drones are all males, and the queen has no more power than any of the others. We listened about how they worked and worked and worked and worked until they eventually died. Their life cycle came to an end in the middle of endless work.

Is it possible to make something so sweet and so lovely, and yet never enjoy the satisfaction of what you've created? Can you miss the opportunity to taste and see the goodness in front of you because you are too fixated on making more goodness you may never experience? I knew it to be true.

Everything surrounding my life testified of my ability to produce goodness, while I continued to choose to choke down the bitter. My adventurous boys would be in the yard discovering grasshoppers, while I chose to stay seated in my lawn chair checking email. Lying in bed beside my husband, being held by strong arms and caressed by a love built on friendship, I'd wonder if he noticed the extra pounds I'd put on. Sweet offerings invited me to taste and see. I set goodness aside for now in hope I'd remember to get a taste tomorrow. As often as these scenarios played out in my days, I spent most of my time choosing the bitter over the sweet. This was a problem, and the only viable solution was to begin sampling what I had been missing.

The secret is in the tasting. Once you get a taste of a well-rested life, nothing else will satisfy. The purpose of rest is not simply so you can get a good night's sleep and wake up refreshed. The purpose of rest is to give you opportunities to taste the life you've created. If life is a gift

how often do we work for the good and put off tasting for someday?

we get to unwrap, rest is the invitation to the celebration worthy of this gift. Rest invites every burned-out, worn-out, tired individual to discover their life's splendor.

Work without the benefit of enjoyment kills the spirit. It is a gift from God for one to find enjoyment in the work. When you're finishing a project or completing a task, don't forget to enjoy it. Accept enjoyment as part of doing a job well. Failure to see goodness leads to an endless cycle of dissatisfaction. You'll never find happiness if you major in producing goodness and minor in experiencing it. There are parts of your life that glisten like honey from the comb. Can you perceive them? Or are you too busy focusing on the work yet to be done? Seek to taste the sweet, and in the process, you'll find your life.

Secrets of the Well Rested

A well-rested life is a secret hidden in plain sight. It is a life at one with God, self, and others. It's a life strengthened by winding down the expectations of others and charging up your expectations for yourself. You become in tune with what you need to be at your best. You become comfortable with your strengths and knowledgeable about your weaknesses. You then use that information to pour into the areas needing strengthening and reinforce areas already strong. You find your sweet spot in living, loving, being, doing, and resting.

Once you find your sweet spot, you land there. You set some personal ground rules on how to best care for yourself so that you can be your best for others. You confidently answer no to requests that fail to be your best yes. As rest restores your body, mind, and spirit, you will begin to experience the secret life of the well rested.

In particular, I've noticed seven secrets of the well rested born out of a life fixated on the reality of the *power of rest* to unlock the gifts inside them. Follow these to your own well-rested life:

1. Don't bend your life to fit into a space too small for your personal needs. You may break in the process.

2. More is only better if you already have a system for releasing the overflow. Otherwise, the abundance will hinder your ability to move freely.

3. Your only limits are the mental ties you allow to bind you. Thinking differently precedes doing differently.

4. Truth is the ultimate healing elixir. Spend time seeking it to undo the damage of debilitating lies.

5. When you step out of the familiar into something new, expect to stumble along. Uncharted territory may feel unstable, but it is capable of bearing the weight of your advancement.

6. The war against fatigue in your mind, body, and spirit is won through submission. What you lay down on purpose today gains potential power for the future.

7. The power to overcome busy is hidden in the depths of surrender. Not giving up freedom or relinquishing anything of value, but releasing the heaviness of too much so you can enjoy a well-rested life.

In the next section, we will discuss the twelve gifts of a well-rested life. I encourage you to consider participating in my Sacred Rest Challenge to help you apply what you've learned in the first section. The challenge is made up of a daily Sacred Rest assignment for thirty consecutive days. As with Karen in chapter 2, I'm offering to walk the journey with you. To the ones who have never found rest, may you enter into rest. To the ones who once did rest but now do not, may you return to rest. To the ones who are currently enjoying rest, may you endeavor to keep it sacred.

PART II

THE GIFTS OF REST

"Every good and perfect gift is from above."

JAMES 1:17 NIV

Chapter 13

The Gift of Boundaries

The plans have been set on the schedule for weeks. Today is your day for soul-care. You need this, your body and your mind need this. You pull into the car line to drop the kids off at school. You wave as a friend approaches your car. Someone has canceled helping out at today's book fair. She needs volunteers. It's only one hour, you reason, so you say yes. One hour turns into two and before you know it you've spent half your day sorting Dr. Seuss and Diary of a Wimpy Kid books. There is still time. You just need to grab a few things at the market for dinner before you take a rest. And the market is right by the dry cleaners, so you might as well swing by there to grab your items. Inside the supermarket, you spot a book on the stand. You remember you have book club tomorrow and you haven't finished the book yet. Oh, and you almost forgot—you still need to wrap your mom's birthday present before you take her out to lunch tomorrow. Tonight will have to be a late one to get everything done. You glance at your watch to find you have one hour before you need to pick the kids up from school. One hour of soul time is better than nothing, right? You'll take it. But just as you settle into a comfortable chair to pray and relax, your cell phone rings. Your sister just has to tell you about the drama she had this morning with a coworker. She needs to talk, so you listen. Forty-five minutes later, you find yourself dashing to the school. You grab a Hershey's Kiss off the counter as you leave. A little chocolate for the soul is all you have time for before getting one child to soccer practice and the other to piano lessons. After picking everyone up, you head home to throw together dinner. The pasta sauce simmers as you help work through algebra on one side of the kitchen table and biology on the other. Two hours later, the meal is finished, the table is cleared, and the kids head to bed. The only soul-care left for today is sleep. Another well-intended day devoured by too many yeses.

Rest is not a luxury; it's a necessity. It is needed to be able to give into the lives of those you care for. So why do we find it so difficult to say no when asked to help a friend out, volunteer our time, or do something we don't feel like doing at that moment? Does the work need to be done? Absolutely. Work will always need to be done. There will always be activities and good things requiring your attention, but all those things can't take precedence over what you need to feel well rested. What steals your rest? Answering this question helps reveal the benefits of having boundaries and the gift we have in setting boundaries within our lives.

Personal boundaries help define your identity. Boundaries create space between you and others. They allow you to know your own place within every relationship. They are the lines clearly demarcated around your body, emotions, mind, and spirit showing where your personal space begins and ends, and how it intersects with that of others. Boundaries help us see what we value. They require you to take a good look at what you need, what you believe, how you feel, and what you require to feel secure, loved, and respected. When we lack these defining boundaries, we are more apt to relinquish control of our day, our activities, and our yeses.

BOUNDARIES

Good boundaries help you to build stronger relationships. They protect you from becoming distracted and manipulated into others' agendas. They prevent you from being led by your insecurities. Boundaries stabilize you and provide a foundation for you to help others honor your basic needs. Personal boundaries are not about being selfish. They are about self-care and understanding your own limitations and accessibility. Loosely defined boundaries are the reason many find themselves stressed out and emotionally depleted. When we are ineffective in setting limits with others, we open the door for hurt feelings and unnecessary relational stress as well as strain our physical, emotional, social, mental, and spiritual resources. These resources are depleted every time we give a begrudging yes when we really mean no. Every time we avoid being authentic and speaking truth to others, every time we are afraid to let people know we have exceeded our limits and we have nothing else to offer. So rather than an honest no, we give a polite yes. A yes that's far from our best. A yes that embodies everything we are trying to escape, all for the sake of not injuring another with our truth. But what is more damaging: a resentful yes or a heartfelt no? What inflicts more pain: speaking the truth in love or speaking a lie to deceive? Is it their feelings we are trying to spare, or is it our desire to not risk testing a relationship with truth?

Healthy boundaries have a healthy relationship with personal truth. When you attempt to rescue your family and friends from having to accept your boundaries, you create opportunities for others to hurt you by enabling them to become more selfish in how they interact with you. Your boundaries will not please everyone. Boundaries are by definition confrontational. They are demarcations on your life to show others how far they can go with you. They are lines in the sand that reveal what you will and will not tolerate. And they are guidelines to help you see when you're getting off track and when others are no longer respecting your set limits.

In the past, the main reason I avoided saying no was I didn't want to feel guilty about disappointing or upsetting someone. What I didn't anticipate is it is just as detrimental to upset and disappoint yourself by making choices that do not represent your heart. Learn to say no with grace. Be sympathetic to your soul and have mercy on yourself by enforcing your rest boundaries. Prioritize those people and things that you want to come first and hold fast to your conviction to live your priorities.

Some of the sweetest people I know have no clear personal boundaries. They include the friend you call upon at the last minute to help you because you know she will drop everything to do it. This is the person you know will give you a yes, even if a reluctant one. You may be that person. You may be the one everyone depends on to step in when others step out. Your number may be the one on speed dial to receive a last-minute call to make brownies for tomorrow's bake sale or an early morning text to help build a science fair booth. There's nothing wrong with being helpful when it fits your values, your priorities, your energy, your gifts, and your passion. But there is something wrong with saying yes for reasons that have nothing to do with your heart's desires and everything to do with the fear of letting someone else down.

I can relate to these people-pleasing qualities. I've seen the people-pleaser in me fight to maintain unbalanced relationships. I too have said yes to many things I never wanted to do. I remember one evening standing in the kitchen near tears trying to complete a project for my son's class. The teacher asked if I would help her out by doing it. I found myself saying an unhappy yes. One thing I am not is an arts and crafts type. I was the last person who should've been in charge of this project. I found myself mixing up a sticky goo to construct the class volcano for science class. By the time the red dye had stained nine of my ten fingers, I no longer cared about being helpful or keeping a smile on my face when I carried this contraption into the classroom. I was hot and fiery enough for me and the volcano, both ready to erupt.

A life secured by personal boundaries is confident and resonates with your values. It is energized by your choices and aligns with your priorities. Boundaries in rest relate to understanding the reasons behind every yes and what differentiates a yes within your boundaries from one outside of your boundaries. Any yes given out of fear, shame, guilt, or insecurity should be a no. Let your yes be yes, and your no be no. Anything more than this comes of evil (see Matt. 5:37). Your boundary lifelines are reinforced when you define your limitations and accept the truth about what is needed to restore and revive your life. It is healthy to prioritize your personal needs, sometimes even over the needs of those you care for. Don't expect others to give you permission to take care of yourself. Know what is required for you to put your best self out there to do the things you were meant to do, and be bold in guarding your life against invasion.

Don't wait until the small foxes have crept in and have your treasures in their grasp before you decide to secure the territory. Start analyzing your personal boundaries now to determine how well they keep the good inside and block what you don't want to allow into your life. What are qualities, relationships, and experiences you put a high priority on? What is it you want to protect? Stress or happiness? Anger or joy? Tension or peace? Foxes are sly; they ravage the valuable and leave behind the remains for you to deal with. Boundaries are how you protect the fruitful areas of your life from becoming burned out, depleted, and exhausted. Every yes out of obligation is like a thief sneaking into your field eating away at the fruit of your life, each weakening you and making it harder to sustain the fullness you are capable of holding.

Your life was never designed to be lived in constant depletion. You are not designed to withstand continuous pouring out with no plan for regular replenishment. How do you respond to daily rest interruptions? What is your reply when others push against your personal boundaries? Often I find in these situations I'm prone to go on the defense. I defend my reasons for rest. I fight against the temptress trying to pull me back into more work. A defensive life leads to unnecessary energy expenditure. Those most successful at living well rested are those who are proactive in pursuing a lifestyle of rest. Their boundaries are formed around life-enriching moments with the power to give back energy, grace, intimacy, and focus. They treasure what's important for the sanctity of their rest, and they do so without apology. It means sometimes you will disappoint people. It means being truthful even when it may not feel comfortable. It means standing up for the rest your soul needs.

Rest boundaries are not only healthy; they are also holy and sacred. As a physician, I'm often drawn to the Gospel as written by Luke, who was also in the medical profession. Medicine in those days was still focused on healing and making people whole in every area of their life. It wasn't about prescribing pills; it was about prescribing life. Luke dissected the life of Jesus as one looking for the fountain of all happiness, joy, and peace. He reveals the inner workings of a well-rested life by sharing personal boundaries Jesus placed within his own life. These boundaries align with the seven types of rest we discussed in the first section of this book.

It often feels as if there's way too much to do, but some of the things occupying our to-do list are not part of God's will for our lives. Our intentions may be pure, and our desire may be to please Him, yet He cannot be pleased watching us work ourselves to death. Much of the pressure we feel to do more and be more is not coming from God but from our own ambitions, from employers, from family, or from friends. Consider Jesus' examples of sacred rest boundaries as you start looking at the boundaries you place around your time, your availability, and your activities. Evaluate how you value your personal needs. Determine if there are some weak boundary lines you need to rebuild. With each boundary you establish, you gain a better understanding of your identity and self-worth.

Sacred Rest Boundaries

Emotional boundaries protect you from others' abuse. Jesus resisted against a crowd that was trying to throw Him off a cliff for claiming to be the Messiah (see Luke 4:28–30).

Sensory boundaries protect you from fatigue and overstimulation. Jesus often withdrew from the crowds to desolate places to pray (see Luke 5:15–16).

Physical boundaries protect your health. As the New International Version states, "One day Jesus said to his disciples, 'Let us go over to the other side of the lake.' So they got into a boat and set out. As they sailed, he fell asleep" (Luke 8:22–23).

Social boundaries protect you from the perfectionism trap. When faced with hundreds of hungry people, Jesus extended grace. He did not make an excuse for the meager meal He had to offer his dining guest. No, He took the five loaves and the two fish and looked up to heaven, blessed them, broke them into pieces and passed them to His disciples to serve to the crowds. Everybody ate and was satisfied. (See Luke 9:10–17.)

Social boundaries also value your inner circle. Jesus took Peter, John, and James, His three closest friends, on a mountain to pray and there He revealed truth (see Luke 9:28).

Spiritual boundaries provide room for unhurried intimacy. When asked what is the greatest commandment, Jesus answered, " 'Love the Lord your God with all your heart and with all your soul and with all your strength and with all your mind'; and, 'Love your neighbor as yourself.' " (Luke 10:27 NIV).

Mental boundaries protect your priorities. Jesus said, "No one can serve two masters. Either he will hate the one and love the other, or he will be devoted to the one and despise the other" (Luke 16:13 ESV).

Creative boundaries abandon life's outcomes to God's sovereignty. Jesus was tempted to be overcome with fear about the cross. He overcame by letting go. He chose not to force things, but to trust God's will. He said, "Father, if you are willing, take this cup from me; yet not my will, but yours be done" (Luke 22:42 NIV).

Chapter 14

The Gift of Reflection

A pond sits outside my home. Sometimes as I stare out my kitchen window, I catch a glimpse of the local wildlife as they come to drink. On one rare occasion, a small herd of deer wandered into the yard. I watched in amazement as seven deer grazed on the lush green grass surrounding the water, each taking turns to keep watch for predators. The youngest held back, staying close to his mother. Eventually, he approached the water's edge and walked in. The excitement of the experience seemed to overtake him. He splashed and danced all around the edge of the pond, kicking up water in all directions. This went on for many minutes. Long after the rest of the herd started to head back into the surrounding woods, this small deer was unhurried. He stood mesmerized at the end of the water while his mama kept watch. I'm not sure what fascinated him so, but during my times standing in that same spot, I too have found myself overwhelmed by what I see in its depths. Just as the surface of the pond displays the beauty of the sky when it is undisturbed, so the soul reflects the image of God when it enters into sacred rest.

Reflecting on life is a gift with the potential to transform and edify. Reflection can be a mirrorlike image bounced back from another surface, or it can describe the process of looking back at a situation or experience.[1] Both definitions refer to going back, one to a prior time and the other to an original image. We are always in need of reflection. Sometimes we need to learn a lesson from the past. And other times the need for reflection arises because we must remember who we are. Standing at the water's edge, I see a reflection of God. Not because I'm perfect and not because I'm holy. This image doesn't come from knowing Scriptures or being able to win at Bible trivia. The reflection of God I see comes from an internal desire to love well. Of all the attributes of God, in all the stories from Genesis to Revelation, the overwhelming theme of the Bible is love. And the gift of reflection allows us to see how well we give and receive love.

The image of God is not reflected in our hectic, frantic schedules. The image of God is not seen in our apathy to the poor and hurting. It is not reflected in our indifference to others. Once our souls become numb, we can no longer see God's reflection in our lives. We feel God has abandoned or left us bankrupt in our weakness and frailty. But He never leaves or forsakes us.[2] Any distance or separation we feel is of our own choice. In choosing to omit rest, we choose to look away from God. A life reflecting God's love is one abounding in rest. It is a life confident in His love and resting in blessed assurance. It emanates from God to others and carries the power of His presence. You have that same power inside. You are an expression of the image of God, a representation of love. Through you, God can do exceedingly and abundantly above all you can ask or think.[3] So look into the water. See the reflection of trees, clouds, and birds in the sky. Then begin to consider your life's reflection of God. What aspect of His character is embedded in your DNA? What part of *thy kingdom come* are you equipped to help His will be done on earth as it is in heaven?

When God finished creating the heavens and the earth, He looked upon His creation and declared it was very good (see Gen. 1:31). Busyness does not lend itself to time for reflection. Reflection is a gift that allows you to look back on your accomplishments. It allows you to discern what worked from what did not, and use that information to move forward stronger than how you began. It is fundamental to personal growth and can be accomplished only in moments of contemplative rest.

Contemplative rest offers opportunities to see how well our lives reflect God's goodness. There are times of introspection so we can evaluate how well we reflect the goodness of God to ourselves, our families, our neighbors, strangers, and even our possessions. As we look into the mirror, we can see if our life is one of reflection or refraction. Refraction is the opposite of reflection. Rather than bouncing back a mirrorlike image, refraction distorts the image. It mimics the original but fails to represent it with accuracy. Refraction deceives; reflection reveals. With reflection, light pierces through the water, hits the surface, then returns an image that is identical to the one from which the light first passed. In refraction, the light again hits the surface but when it returns it changes direction and takes a different path. Be careful of any path leading you away from the light of God.

A Holy Perspective

Recently my son received a telescope from his grandpa for Christmas. We were ecstatic about this gift because in the coming month a series of four lunar eclipses were to occur. Lunar eclipses are an amazing example of reflection. When there's a full moon, the light illuminates the night sky. It reflects back the light from the sun with such intensity that it can create its own shadows from its light. However, when there is a lunar eclipse, the Earth separates the sun and the moon. The moon is still full, but rather than appearing bright, it's dark with deep blood-red undertones. When looking at the sun, the moon reflects its light and brilliance. When looking at the Earth, the moon reflects its darkness and its internal turmoil.[4]

Similarly, when we are looking at the things of God we will reflect His mind and His holy perspective. When our attention shifts to the things of earth, our lives will reflect darkness and depression. We need times of sacred rest scheduled into our busy days so we can turn toward God. We need His gift of reflection so we can be transformed into His likeness and reflect His glory.

How do you see yourself? Looking back on your past choices in life can cause you to define yourself in ways that travel a path of refraction. The light of God comes in through the twisted surface of your memories, and how you see is contrary to what He says. You see guilty; He sees forgiven. You see an outsider; He sees His beloved. You see your mistakes; He sees your redemption. How do we correct these refractions in our spiritual vision?

God sees you from the perspective of all He made you to be. His view of you encompasses all the potential within you. It is a perfect reflection of you. Too often we can see only the negative in ourselves. We are drawn to the weaknesses and imperfections. God does not focus on these things. His view never becomes distorted. Within your weaknesses, He sees you strengthened during your times of spiritual, physical, and emotional rest. In your insecurities, He sees your relationships deepening from your times of social rest. In your past mistakes and failures, He sees you learning and growing during times of creative rest. In your lack of vision, He sees you restored to new sight during your times of sensory rest.

In his research, John Dewey concluded, "We do not learn from experience...We learn from reflecting on experience."[5] In our experiences, the goal is not to become complacent in our successes or defeated by our failures, but to use each as seeds for growth. All seeds germinate best in ground softened by deep watering. Each opportunity to quiet ourselves and to allow time for self-reflection is a moment we can drink deep. Learning from our experiences is not found in the activity or in the action; it is found in meditating on the experience. Reflection moves us from one experience to the next and helps us understand its relationship and its connection to every other experience we've had. Reflection gives us a chance to interact with others through the joining of shared experiences. As we process every experience, it either reveals itself to be a reflection of God or a refractory image. When we look back on life, we can see the lessons learned, witness the answered prayers, and see the dreams that have become reality. Then we can determine what is a reflection and what is a refraction. We keep God's reflection beautiful and radiant in our lives by offering back the good and the holy we have experienced. As our lives testify of God's faithfulness, His reflection permeates through our spirit.

You may be wondering what reflecting the light of God looks like. It looks like loving boldly. It looks like compassion toward those who are mistreated. It looks like concern for the less than and the marginalized. It looks like a dinner table without cell phones. It looks like times of solitude listening to the voice of God. It looks like holding hands with the one you love. It looks like rocking a feverish child while singing a lullaby. It looks like you living rested and whole.

Exodus 34:29–35 tells us that after spending time in the presence of God, Moses' face was radiant, and shone with the reflection of the light of God. It was so bright the people were afraid of him. Time in God's presence has not lost its power. Just as Moses radiated and reflected the glory of God, we can also reflect Him in our day-to-day lives. Not all people will understand the changes they see in you as you embrace a well-rested life. Darkness is always intimidated by light.

Beholding Glory

"But we all, with unveiled face, beholding as in a mirror the glory of the Lord, are being transformed into the same image from glory to glory, just as from the Lord, the Spirit."

2 CORINTHIANS 3:18 NASB

Glory can only be witnessed; it cannot be manufactured. We have no glory, or light, on our own. A mirror cannot reflect light in a dark room until you point it toward a light source. We also cannot reflect something we are not looking at. We can never reflect the glory of God unless we are gazing in His direction. You must experience the glory of God for yourselves. Rest is your appointment with Him. Rest is your opportunity to come face-to-face with the sacredness of life.

The only way to reflect His glory is to stay grounded in His presence—by seeing Him in the big and the small of life. Each day has its share of highs and lows. One friend calls to announce her pregnancy, while another cries into an empty cradle. You watch your graduate take the podium, while anxiety rages in your heart over your empty nest. Life is always changing. We experience our share of successes and losses. In all this, we desperately need rest. We require time to redirect our focus off the darkness and back toward God. During these moments of reflection, we become transformed.

Rest moves us from one level of understanding to the next. It transforms us. Rest is not having to run back again to our old ways of doing things.[6] One way to enjoy the gift of reflection can be to view the old without contempt for the work required to accomplish the needed transition and change. I'm convinced this is how Paul was able to say, "It was good that I was afflicted" (Psalm 119:71 NIV). He wasn't celebrating the pain, but rather reflecting on the transformation it accomplished in him.

What is it you see when you look at your life today? Analyze everything from your family, your friends, your home, where you live, the work you do, the foods you eat, the positions you value, the places you enjoy, the music you listen to, the books you read, the sports you play, the people you encounter, and the difference you make in the lives of others. If any of these areas do not accurately reflect the abundant life available to you, congratulations! You are in the perfect place to witness your life resurrected. This is the power of rest. It will breathe life into your mind, heart, and spirit as you receive from God. You can experience the rebirth of becoming a new creation in Christ. Begin by seeing what God sees in you and take note of the areas that do not reflect His kingdom coming on earth as it is in heaven. See refraction for the lie that it is and redirect your focus back to the light of God. Be a gift reflecting the glory you behold.

Chapter 15

The Gift of Freedom

I begin each January by picking a word of the year, a single word that I will use as my focal point to direct what I hope to learn during the next twelve months. Some of my words for the year have been *love*, *faith*, *joy*, and *peace*. I love when my word comes with a promise attached. Then one year the word I felt compelled to use was one I didn't want to touch. It was one of those words that make you pause and consider if you are ready to go there. That word was *surrender*.

What woman doesn't enjoy companionship on a journey? Especially a journey that sounds like it may require a shoulder to lean on, or maybe cry on. I invited a few hundred ladies to join me on my journey to find out what would happen if we surrendered all those things we hold dear—three weeks, twenty-one days, to uncover the things we hold back from God and prayerfully surrender each into His care. I expected it to be difficult, but what I didn't expect was for it to turn into twenty-one days of intense spiritual battle. Problems, issues, and unfavorable circumstances became daily occurrences. Every prayer seemingly shot down by an unseen foe. Every offering devoured before the seed could bloom. My desire to be free was under attack.

Surrender sounds like such an easy process. We have all seen movies where people surrender. Criminals surrender to police and prisoners of war surrender to their captors. The universal sign of surrender is the same sign we each practice during times of worship with both hands extended up into the air. Unlike the criminal, we are not pleading our guilt. We trust that Jesus paid it all on the cross and we are now redeemed in the eyes of God. And unlike the prisoner of war, we are not surrendering to give up our individuality, but rather as a way to better understand who we are. We are not surrendering to subtract from our lives, but to open ourselves to receive even more. We surrender to the love of God, the power of that love, and its ability to change us and change how we view our circumstances. Surrender is the process through which we gain all.

Work for many of us has become a burden. Careers we have trained hard to secure have turned into a ball and chain we feel tethered to for life. We were never intended to be enslaved to any type of bondage, including the bondage of our overextended schedules and maxed-out lives. Slaves are bound to their work. Anyone who cannot rest is essentially a slave. Jesus came to set the captives free so that we may have abundant life.[1] Sacred rest is about that freedom.

Since God is really the only one able to love us on the level our hearts desire, we are constantly seeking the wholeness, peace, joy, and happiness that can be found only in this place of surrender. Rest is knowing that you are enough, even if you don't meet your goal this month. It's knowing that you are valuable as you are with no additions needed. Rest is knowing that you are preapproved for all of God's blessings. It's knowing that you are not in competition with others. Rest is knowing that your worst day is still in God's hands. Rest is knowing the limitlessness of the Almighty. This is what living well rested looks like. It's a life lived with open hands before God, not holding on to the pain of yesterday, the blessings of today, or the promises of tomorrow, but rather trusting in God's love for you. Living well rested is a life surrendered to the gift of freedom. There is freedom available to anyone with the audacity to trust God's ways and enter into His rest.

When God is trying to take you into a new place in Him, it requires your yes and it calls you to surrender your desire, your will, and your plan. For most of us, living well rested is a new place in God. It's a place we long to be but have not been able to enter. We are like the Israelites in the exodus. We have applied the blood of the lamb to the doorposts, and we have left Egypt.[2] We are no longer in the bondage of our past, but we now stand in a new place of bondage. We stand in the wilderness somewhere between the busy woman we used to be and the restful woman we desire to be. We see the giants in the land and fear if we lose all our baggage in this unknown place, we may not recognize the woman we become. So the fear of living well rested keeps us locked in our perceived comfort zones. But then again they aren't so comfortable, are they?

I recall recently seeing a beautiful birdcage with a tiny bird singing happily behind its bars at a local pet store. Matthew 10:31 teaches us that God's eye is on the sparrow and that He has not forgotten even one of these little birds. You are even more important to Him. He sees you in your own beautiful places of confinement, and although there are times you feel content in this place you are at, the part of you that was created to fly with Him knows that there is so much more He desires to show you. He doesn't just want to open the door long enough for you to fly in and out of His rest. God wants to see every part of you set free to rest in Him. He desires entry into every hidden part of you, every treasure you have found, and every pain you would rather forget. These are the doors in your heart He desires to open. Once they are open, you can be free from the limiting effects these things had on you. Notice some of these things may be your greatest blessings and others your worst nightmare. All of them stand between you and the open door God has for you. These are the things that have to be surrendered to enter into the freedom of God.

Let's be honest with each other. I'm sure some of you have not been able to enjoy rest despite your best efforts. How do I know this? Because I've been there. I know what it's like to want to be happy but feel stress and anxiety pushing against my peace. I know what it's like to pray and pray and pray and feel like God has turned a deaf ear to my request. I know what it feels like when joy doesn't come in the morning, holding tight to the Scriptures, but they do not appear to be alive and working. You find yourself beating on the chest of God with a clenched fist, holding on so tight to His promises that you can't feel His embrace. I've been there, and the lesson I learned was that it wasn't about me doing more, but rather about me learning how to surrender. Because while I was beating on His chest, all He wanted to do was love on me. It's hard to rest in the arms of someone you're fighting back against.

Five Steps to Surrender to the Gift of Freedom

1. Acknowledge the sovereignty of God.

Sovereignty means that God, as the ruler of the universe, has the right to do whatever He wants. He doesn't have to get our approval or permission to be who He is. Acknowledging this means we must recognize all His attributes. It means seeing Him as the Almighty God, as the God who is above all things without limitation, as the Creator of heaven and earth, the Maker of all things, the One with the power to perform miracles, signs, and wonders, the God for whom nothing is impossible. He who is able to do exceeding abundantly above all that we ask or think.

When you get a better understanding of who God is, you quickly realize the act of surrender is just a change in mind-set. We really never have possession over the things we claim possession to. What we are truly surrendering are our anxious thoughts about those things, our fears, doubts, and unbelief in exchange for the freedom to rest in His sovereignty.

2. Cease fighting to have your way.

Romans 9:20 says, "But who are you, a human being, to talk back to God? 'Shall what is formed say to the one who formed it, "Why did you make me like this?"'" (NIV). Ouch! I love and hate this passage of Scripture at the same time. I've had this conversation with God more times than I can count. "God, why did you make me like this?" Has anyone else been there? Upset with God about some aspect of my personality. Praying God will change a situation that He seems perfectly content with.

When we don't understand what God is doing, we journey into the battlefield of the mind and wage a war against our circumstances in the hopes that if we try hard enough and fight long enough, we will overcome the difficulty. But this is not the gift of freedom. Freedom is this: Instead of trying harder, trust more. Cease fighting, and with hands raised, bow your will to His. Assume a position of peace even in the midst of unfavorable circumstances or unknown outcomes. One way you know you've surrendered and ceased fighting is when you don't immediately react to adversity or challenging circumstances with fear and anxiety. You let go of your need to struggle and allow God to fight on your behalf. Some battles were never yours to fight standing, but the Lord's to fight while you rest.

3. Let go of your need to control the outcome.

I used to really dislike the saying "let go and let God" because I didn't want to let go. I wanted to hold on for dear life, and if God wanted to work out a good outcome, then He was welcome to do so while I held on tight. My fear was that if I let go and released the outcome to God, I might not like what He decides. But sometimes the lines can get blurry, and it can be difficult to determine what we really need to release and what we need to hold on to. We can quickly spot negative things we need to let go of like a lack of forgiveness or shame, but what about those times when the thing we need to let go of is actually something good? Courageous rest is needed to let go and live free. Every good gift in your life is not a final resting place. There are times when we have to let go of what we think is good because God has something better for us. Then there are also times when we must give up our preconceived notions of how life should be and accept that God will occasionally ask us to walk some tough roads so that we can grow and mature to become stronger in our faith.

4. Rest in the knowledge of the goodness of God.

The question that has arisen in the mind of every believer is, "Can I trust God?" For most of my adult life, the answer was no. I didn't trust God. How could a good God allow my mom to die in childbirth? I couldn't rest in the knowledge of His goodness because I didn't believe He had been good to me. It didn't seem fair. Every time I thought about what I missed, what we as a family missed, *good* was not the word that came to mind. To make matters worse, I grew up in the Bible Belt where people said things like, "God needed your mother more." "God needed an angel in Heaven." "God loved her more." So to me God was not good, He was selfish.

When you harbor those types of feelings about God, it's impossible to surrender to the gift of freedom. You can't surrender to someone you don't trust. You can love God and still not trust God. So how do you get to the place in your walk with God where you trust Him? It starts by first acknowledging the obvious: Life is not always good. Bad things do happen. Since we already established that we serve a sovereign God, He obviously is aware of these events before they touch your life. So how can you trust Him if He allows unfavorable circumstances to enter your life? You trust that He is who He says He is. When Moses was headed to Egypt to confront Pharaoh, he asked God, "Who shall I say sent me?" and God replied, "I AM WHO I AM."[3]

I AM is a name that takes into account everything that is missing and broken in your life. I can say I trust God now because when sorrow comes, His spirit whispers, "I AM your Comforter." I can say I trust God now because when pain, illness, or injury touches my family, I AM is our healer. Some are healed on this side of heaven and some on the other like my mother, but God's goodness does not change with that position. In the middle of every situation, good or bad, He simply states, "I AM WHO I AM." So bad things still happen, and I don't always like the outcome of situations, but His goodness remains intact because my circumstances do not change who He is. I can trust Him, and I can rest in His goodness, even when goodness is not what I'm experiencing at the moment. It comes back to surrendering to His love for you and believing Romans 8:28—that all things work together for good. Not just the good things, but *all* things.

5. Decrease so God can increase in your life.

Matthew 10:39 says, "If you cling to your life, you will lose it; but if you give up your life for me, you will find it" (NLT). Genuine surrender says, "Father, if this problem, pain, sickness, or circumstance is needed to fulfill your purpose and glory in my life, don't take it away! I will trust You in this situation and depend on Your strength when I feel weak." This is not an easy statement. Even Jesus struggled with this. In Mark 14:36 He cried, "Father, everything is possible for you. Please take this cup of suffering away from me. Yet I want your will to be done, not mine" (NLT).

Decreasing is part of surrendering. It moves God back into His proper position as lord of your life. It places Him back on the throne and dislodges any idols that have tried to claim His place. There are lots of idols that fight for position in our hearts, and some are so subtle they take center stage and set up house long before we realize they're trying to replace the real King of kings and Lord of lords. When your idols have surrendered, and you are no longer weighed down by their clutter, then you can receive the gift of freedom.

This is the process to living free. When you've tried all you know to do, and it feels like you will never be able to rest in God...surrender.

Chapter 16

The Gift of Acceptance

My thirtysomething life looked a lot like the overcooked brownies I'd just pulled out of the oven: dry, hard, and begging for someone to turn off the heat. The fire and drive to succeed, an asset in one season of my life, turned into a hot mess in the next. Work became how I proved my worth. It became my preferred emotional fix, and it sustained my need to please. It allowed daily stamps of approval in the form of completed tasks, accomplished goals, and words of affirmation. As I stared into the pan of burnt brownies, I began to see things about my life I could notice only when gazing into ruined chocolate.

I am prone to overdo things. I overplan every family trip. I overswing the club when playing miniature golf. I overshoot the basket when playing hoops with my boys. I overfertilize the flowers in my garden. I do everything to the utmost. I am a chronic overcompensator. I take to the extreme those situations that are content being small. Small looks too weak to be of any substantial value. Small intimidates me. It stands in contrast to what I believe success looks like, but small is part of a balanced life.

All any life wants is to find balance. Where there is no inclination for the scales to swing in the direction of balance, there is an indication of a life without rest, a life without moments of smallness. My scales were tipped in favor of an overloaded agenda because of an underaffirmed life. I strived to build a reputation as one who accomplished much when all I really wanted was to know I was loved much.

The desire to overwork is an attempt to justify ourselves. For many, there is a connection between our overachieving and our desire to prove our self-worth. Our overcompensating becomes a way to validate our existence. We pour ourselves into our surroundings, into our people, and into our agendas. We add to the productivity, the creativity, and the humanity of our world, and we do so with a hidden soul-level motive. If we can do enough, we can be enough. Oh, how the soul loves to war with the spirit, for the spirit is proof enough of our worth. Our eternal nature created in the image of God is an affirmation beyond anything our mind and heart could ever comprehend. This is the gift of acceptance, the freedom to live unattached to the validation of others when you are already preapproved by God. Instead of overreaching for some unknown life purpose, you come boldly into the place of God's grace in your life.

One beautiful September evening, I found myself sitting with my friend Paisley in a corner deli in Philadelphia. Paisley and I were best friends throughout high school. We grew apart over the years because of distance, kids, and hectic career schedules, but we reconnected on social media. I reached out to her while I was in town for a conference. Over cheesesteaks stuffed high with sautéed peppers and onions, we discussed finding life's purpose.

"If we each have a destiny and a purpose to fulfill, why does God make it so difficult to find?" I asked. "Purpose has become the journey of a thousand unknowns. If I knew what God wanted me to do, I could do it and then have time to get on with my life."

I don't believe living a purpose-driven life is supposed to feel like a game of Monopoly—roll the dice and hope you land on Boardwalk. Yet this was my experience. Purpose was a gray zone in the unde-fined areas of my black-and-white life. Purpose was another goal to be obtained. The goal setter in me wanted to knock it out of the park and move on, but purpose won't allow you to move on. You can't move on from who you are. You and your purpose are inseparable, intertwined for eternity. Purpose is the DNA of your soul, knit into you from the moment of conception. It is the pattern from which everything about you originates. You don't find purpose. You live and let purpose reveal itself to you. Just as every renowned artist, musician, or writer had to begin with a first brushstroke, note, and word, every purpose-filled life must begin with a first encounter with your why.

I equated living on purpose with doing things for a purpose. There are many wonderful life-giving, life-changing, world-shaping activi-ties I can do, but only a few will align with my purpose. Everything else is wind in the storm. It was time for me to separate the wheat from the chaff in my life. I needed to determine those things I did because they were mine to do and the things I did because I wanted to please others.

I wholeheartedly believe working hard is important to life and existence. Successful people are often the product of an overachiev-ing lifestyle. But while overachieving can build a career, I'm not con-vinced it can create an internal awareness of your self-worth or lead to a clear understanding of purpose. You are made for something bigger than your schedule or your ability to get things done. You are made to live within the wide-open space of God's validation and affirmation. You are made to abide in the gift of acceptance.

When there is nothing left to prove and no "attagirl" accolades left to earn, what will your motivation be to push harder, work longer, and fight stronger? I spent more time fighting this battle than necessary, fist-punching the air at finding my purpose so I could achieve the great things God put me on this earth for, when all the while He stood waiting for me to put my arms down to receive the embrace of acceptance I desired. This gift of acceptance is not the reward of living a purposeful life; it is the resting place from which the confidence to live purpose-driven is birthed.

With every birth there is a breaking of water, and in this breaking we pierce through into a new identity—new to us, but not new to God. We see through the glass darkly where He sees it in full light. Even Jesus had to break through the waters of identity, once through the womb of Mary and once through the baptismal waters of the Jordan. Before the blind could see and the lame walked, He dripped wet from the water, soaked in acceptance. God declared over the place the drops fell, "This is my Beloved Son in whom I am well pleased."[1] His identity was made secure by acceptance, the very same as yours.

The greatest challenge upon accepting this gift is withstanding the counterattack on your identity. Rest assured there will be one, and it will come in the form of an if/then proposition.

If you are _____, then why don't you _____ (see Matt. 4: 1–7).

It's a request designed to call out the overachiever in you. "Come on, show off your power," it will provoke. "Reveal what you are capable of, hot stuff." Don't fall into the trap of approval. Resist. It's a trick to get you to revert back to needing to prove something, to validate your claim on your purpose and your identity. Combat the temptation by refusing to let go of the gift. Let every life-giving affirmation speak courage, strength, and hope into you. Find security in the knowledge you are fearfully and wonderfully made. Unlock the passion of knowing you are irreplaceable, a treasure beloved of God. This is the soul-deep rest of a purpose-filled life. Because of your acceptance, you are free to achieve, succeed, and do greater works in whatever way that may manifest. Your life ceases being about the magnitude of work done and more about the meaning of the work you are doing.

You can rest in smallness, and you can rest in greatness. Each has a time and a season designed for you to prosper. Get out of season, and rest will turn into unrest. In the smallness of the nursery, a baby is rocked to sleep. A bond is formed in the warmth of body to body, a baby's listening ear to a mother's loving heart. On a conference stage, a speaker shares transparently from her own mistakes. In the audience, wounded emotions are bathed in the balm of an encouraging word. A connection is formed between the listening ear of the hurting and the loving heart of the vulnerable. Contentment can be found in every season, whether in obscurity or on a platform. Neither is greater than the other. The magnitude no longer overshadows the meaning. Both are of great value. Both are a part of purpose and identity. Both are a gift.

You are free to participate with God. Free to live, free to move, and free to be (see Acts 17:28). No longer confined to overperforming and overachieving. Resting in the smallness and in the greatness. No longer overplanning family time, free to participate in the spontaneity of living well. Possessing the boldness to fertilize where you desire abundant harvest. No longer pushing the limits demanding your way, but participating in the delicate exchange between faith and action. Working from a place of being acknowledged, affirmed, and approved. This is work under grace. Work born from the rest of being intimately known and accepted (see Ps. 139:1–6).

Chapter 17

The Gift of Exchange

During a recent Skype conversation a friend confided, "My life no longer fits." Her statement hung untouched for several minutes. It needed no further explanation. I had been there when her husband left. I had watched as her familiar setting became a distant memory, and she was left picking up the pieces of her broken dreams. Some life events burn everything in their path. They leave us emotionally and spiritually homeless, desperately looking in our mental backpacks for something that fits. She had reached inside her pack and come up empty-handed.

Empty can be a good place to start. When we come to the end of our abilities, we find God patiently waiting. We empty out our fatigue, frustrations, disappointments, unanswered prayers, heartaches, hurts, and grief. He removes the weight of these burdens, and He pours in healing peace and strength. As you embrace rest as a way of life, you will find yourself getting lighter. You'll laugh more easily, love more deeply, and live more fully. Rest will lift your spirits to a new level of happiness. This is the kind of rest Jesus gives—rest of the deepest, truest kind, rest that the world can't give, and that the world can't possibly take away. When He gives rest, it is precious because it comes from His own hand put into your hand so you can tuck it into your heart.[1]

Rest is a divine exchange. You can bring your stressed-out, tired self and exchange the heaviness of your week for whatever you're lacking. You give God your fatigue; He quiets your body and gives sweet sleep. You lay down your fears and anxieties; He fills your heart with peace. You give God your doubts; He gives you confidence and faith. A trade takes place between soul and spirit. The soul is insatiable till it finds rest. Only then can it recline on the holy and find peace that transcends all understanding.

Jesus beckons us in Matthew 11:28–29 (NIV), "Come to me, all you who are weary and burdened, and I will give you rest. Take my yoke upon you and learn from me, for I am gentle and humble in heart, and you will find rest for your souls." This verse was written for people like you and me, the weary and burdened. Those who are busy being busy and feel we don't have time for rest. It's an invitation to exchange. Jesus invites us *all* without exception: young or old, rich or poor, blue-collar or white-collar, saint or sinner. All the tired, drained, weary, and burdened are welcome to come. Then in His invitation, He offers a gift: "I will give you rest." But to receive the gift, you will need to listen to Jesus, who says, "Come to me...Learn from me." He offers rest, not cessation from work. In His rest there is peace, fulfillment, and a sense of fitting properly.

I once heard a story that helped me understand the imagery in this passage. Jesus grew up in the household of Joseph, a carpenter. It is said in this story that Jesus was gifted and skilled in carpentry. Carpenters create the yokes that go on the backs of animals to help them work more efficiently. It is rumored Jesus made some of the best yokes in Jerusalem. His yokes were smooth and did not irritate the skin of the backs they were placed on. They fit perfectly and allowed the one wearing them to do the specific work for which they were designed.

This is what living should feel like. When we expectantly enter into rest, we can extend our heavy yoke to the Lord of Rest and receive His yoke of restoration, purpose, and peace. Expectant rest moves you closer to being still and knowing God is in you, around you, and working through you. We become fitted to do the work we were designed to do, not the work others desire to load upon us.

The divine exchange Jesus offers is not limited. He does not say, "I will give rest to your mind, your body, your emotions, or your relationships." He leaves this gift wrapped for you to explore because He intends to give you rest in every area of your life. It is an invitation without restriction—rest about everything, rest at all times, and rest in every area.

Can you, at least for a few minutes, extend your weariness, your cares, your doubts, your fears to Him? He stands before you now with nail-scarred hands bidding you to come to Him, asking you to trust Him. What has been exhausting you? Lay it down at His feet. Why should you carry what He will carry for you? Give it over to Him today and receive rest for your soul.

What do you need to exchange to go deeper into a restful state?

Life's Exchange Stations

Physical Exchange—Are you weary from your work activities or burdened from the pressures upon you? There are both active and passive sides of pressure, just as there are both active and passive sides of rest. Exchange physical exertion with time to be still. Soak in a warm bath. Get a massage. Lay yourself down.

Relax the tension in your body and enjoy having your hands free to grab hold of the blessing of rest in your life (see Eccles. 4:6).

Mental Exchange—Daily your mind enters into a battle. It wars to stay at peace. It wars to enter into rest. You have to fight for this exchange. Memorize encouraging Scriptures. Replace negative thoughts with positive affirmations. Fight to enter into this rest of the soul. The weapons you must fight with are not the weapons of the world. On the contrary, they have divine power to demolish the mental strongholds trying to keep you out of mental rest (see 2 Cor. 10:4).

Emotional Exchange—When you have anxiety about anything, you have an invitation to exchange. Take every tormenting thought and fear in prayer to God and let your requests be made known. In expectant thanksgiving, anticipate the peace of God, which surpasses all understanding to guard your hearts and your minds (see Phil. 4:6–7).

Spiritual Exchange—Jesus commits Himself wholeheartedly to His Father's will—and invites us to do the same (see Matt. 11:25–30). Those who are tired of life, or weighed down by dead religion, can come to Him for rest. He fits you with the gentle, liberating yoke of the purpose of God in your life. But He doesn't leave you to labor alone; He places this yoke across His shoulders too. He shares the burden with you and uses it to direct your life back to the will of God.[2]

Sensory Exchange—Our hope is renewed when we see and hear from God's perspective. Fill your surroundings with worship, praise, and uplifting Scriptures. Ask God to give you eyes to see yourself and your situation as He sees you. Also allow room in your day for therapeutic silence. Ask God to open your ears to hear the still small voice encouraging and guiding you today (see 1 Kings 19:12).

Social Exchange—Engage with friends who have the qualities you admire and desire. Just as iron sharpens iron, friends sharpen the minds of each other (see Prov. 27:17).

Creative Exchange—When it's difficult to find God in your circumstances, start by looking for Him in His creations. Hike to a hidden waterfall and hear the melody of His song in nature. Marvel over His use of colors in the earth and inhale the fragrant offerings of a garden. Begin by restoring your belief that He is present and accessible. The more you seek, the more you will find in the process (see Matt. 6:33).

My friend, I pray you are not too busy to accept this invitation. "Come to me...and you will find a deep peace and satisfaction that you could never find elsewhere. I have come for you. Come to me."[3]

Chapter 18

The Gift of Permission

Sunday afternoons beg to be enjoyed with family and friends. Nothing excites my family more than filling a backpack, strapping on hiking boots, and heading out onto an unfamiliar wooded trail. Despite being a woman with an unhealthy aversion to all things grassy, I do love the adventure of trailblazing. On one particular Sunday, it was ninety-five degrees outside. In Alabama, you can't discuss temperature without factoring in the humidity. Ninety-five equals way too hot to even think about going outside for a hike. Unfortunately, my family did not agree with my equation. They were packed and ready to explore a newly opened park with a lakeside walking trail near our home.

Weeks earlier we had attended the grand opening. The park had been dedicated to the Native Americans of the Creek Nation who had allowed our community to use their sacred land. The construction of the park and sports complex had suffered long delays because of the permission needed from the elders of the Creek Nation. The burial grounds could not be disturbed, and great care had to be taken to not offend the first people in the area. After years of mapping and remapping the territories, we now stood looking at miles of trails awaiting new Sunday memories.

Our dog Rosie had even insisted on joining in on the festivities. Rosie is not the type of dog you take on long walks. She is a solid white Havanese with a princess attitude. She prances more than she walks, and this trail was going to be two miles in extremely hot weather. I had visions of needing to rearrange things in the backpack halfway through our walk so I could stuff Rosie into it. Nevertheless, she was in the car when we headed to our destination.

I hope dogs are allowed on the trails, I thought. But before I could inquire more, we were at the park and preparing to begin. All concern about having Rosie with us vanished when I saw countless families out on the trails with their dogs. One brave soul was walking six dogs together. The park was a beautiful example of community. The Indian heritage was proudly displayed with teachings on the Creeks and information about how this land had been used over the years. Fourth-grade Alabama history was coming to life for my boys. We climbed to the top of the lookout point before heading back.

On our way out of the park, we noticed a huge sign. When we had entered the park, we came in on the back side where the playground was and had not seen the sign posted at the entrance. There were well over twenty "do nots" listed. DO NOT USE MOTORIZED BIKES OR SCOOTERS ON THE TRAIL. DO NOT LEAVE TRASH ON THE TRAIL. And right in the middle of the sign it read, NO DOGS ALLOWED ON THE TRAIL. I stared down at Rosie playing catch me if you can with a little girl who had approached her. We had just violated rule #8. Over 50 percent of those at the park that day were violating one rule or another.

This isn't the first time I'm guilty of not following the rules. By now you may be thinking I'm a notorious nonconformist, a girl who likes to do things her way come what may. On the contrary, I like the security of knowing I have permission to do something. I question why rules exist. I don't always agree with what I find, but I learn and grow from a lot of interesting perspectives. One rule I spent years overlooking was tucked so deep into a pocket of "thou shall nots" that I didn't even know it was there.

I grew up in church. As a small child, I sat in Sunday school learning about God. He didn't sound like anyone you'd want to spend a lot of time with. Those early lessons described Him like a policeman. He was the enforcer of the laws. He was the one you wanted to stay away from unless you found yourself in a scary situation needing His assistance. His police manual was the Ten Commandments, and as long as you followed those rules, you would stay out of eternal jail. This childlike understanding of the Ten Commandments served me well. Thou shall not steal. Check. Thou shall not kill. Check. Thou shall not cheat on your spouse. Check. All good things to avoid, right?

It would be hard to argue any of the points stated within the Ten Commandments. However, we do it every time we say we don't have time for rest. We stand before the courtroom of heaven and declare we know best what we need for our mind, body, and spirit to thrive. Even as the words fall from our lips, the debris from our tired souls mocks our arrogant declaration.

In Exodus 20:8 we are commanded to remember the Sabbath and keep it holy. This commandment to observe a set-apart time to rest has been overshadowed by all the "thou shall nots." The only commandment urging us to *remember* is the main one we have forgotten. The unending list of things that need to get done stands before us like a drill sergeant barking orders. In the midst of the noise, rest sounds like one more item added to an overwhelming list.

God did not make rest a mere suggestion, He commanded it. Any loving parent knows what is best for their children and will make them go to bed at a reasonable time. Likewise, God looks upon His beloved and whispers to the deep places of your heart, "Rest."

Our twenty-first-century lives reek of exhaustion. We now live longer than our ancestors, but we spend less time living life and more time fighting death. They died quickly from wearing out their bodies; we die slowly from wearing out our minds. We are busy doing, being, and becoming with little regard for the people we ignore and the moments we miss. There is value in work, and there is value in rest; both are vital for a life well lived.

Feeling Unworthy of Rest

The gift of permission removes the guilt associated with rest. Rest is not laziness. Rest is the grace we extend to ourselves. It is the yes of a body surrendering to a holy command. It's an act of obedience. You are not going to stumble into obedience. You have to make a conscious effort to rest on purpose. And those who depend on you to do it all will not be happy about your newfound love of this command.

We often ask others for permission to do things in our life. Can I have time off for Christmas, Boss? Honey, can you watch the kids so I can go to a Zumba class? Our choices and actions are mandated by the people we live with because we need them to live. Time off and time to participate in fun activities is wonderful, but as you have been learning, rest is so much more than just leisure time. You don't need anyone's assistance to turn away from your computer for five minutes, close your eyes, unwind tense muscles, clear your mind, and be still. Help is not required to step outside your home at night for five minutes to experience the evening chill, gaze at the stars, and extend gratitude for the goodness you experienced today. Even if you are a single parent caring for a little one, bundle up your little stargazing companion and enjoy a moment of creative rest together. The only one holding you back from rest is you. Own up to your part in your current rest deficit and accept the gift of permission.

There will be people in your circle who will be quick to unload their exhaustion and guilt right onto your well-rested head. They may or may not even know they are adding to the reason you feel unworthy of rest. When I surveyed men and women on reasons they don't rest, the replies were best summed up by Danielle:

> *No one I know is resting. None of my girlfriends have time for herself. None of our husbands have time to relax. My kids run from school to activities, only to come home and have hours of homework before they fall into bed. If I started resting, I would look like the laziest person on our cul-de-sac.*

Rest ruins our reputation for being superhuman. Rest testifies to our humanity and our need for daily replenishing—our need for daily bread. The breaking of this bread is a difficult task for those malnourished from years of fasting from rest. Bite by bite, that's the only way to digest dense matter. If you try to keep up with a sprinting society on a diet of crumbs, you're going to end up more than physically exhausted. You'll be mentally scattered, emotionally chunked, and spiritually smothered. Sounds like a hash brown order at Waffle House but significantly more damaging to your health.

Permission for sacred rest has already been granted. The question is, will you remember to keep it holy?

Chapter 19

The Gift of Cessation

A recent bout of ice and snow in my area left the streets glossy and dangerous. Salt and sand covered the major roads to help us busy people continue working, doing, and producing. Who has time for a snow day except kids, right? I've learned people in the South do not keep their doctors' appointments when snow is on the ground. If the meteorologist even hints at the thought of flurries, southerners go into hibernation mode.

Thankfully, this influx of winter weather changed to spring within a week. We spent Sunday drinking hot chocolate to fight off the nineteen-degree temperature outside, and by Saturday the kids were back in shorts and T-shirts playing basketball and sweating in the seventy-five-degree heat. The residue of winter, however, lingered on my car, and I was desperate to have the salt and sand washed away. As I found my place to the front of the automatic car wash line, the attendant reminded me to shift into neutral.

I need this reminder in my daily life as well.

This is the gift of cessation, the ability to take our hands off the wheel. It's the ability to stop, not because you are exhausted and have to, but because you choose to. You consciously determine doing nothing is the best next response. We all need neutral moments in our fast-paced lives. Times to disengage from activities and be content in just being. Times of cessation so we can honor our need for relaxation. Most of us feel we have to do something all the time, and many of us think we should be doing something even when we don't have anything we have to do. Cessation is not about stopping all activity. Assuming you're not dead, you're always doing something. When you receive the gift of cessation, you've decided you don't need to justify your existence through pointless activities and can delight in rest. What do you need to cease doing to allow room for intentional rest?

Right about now you may be thinking: *I do rest on the weekends.* But do you really? If you fill your weekends with errands, laundry, yard work, and scheduled activities, this is not rest. Rest should change you for the better. You can identify rest by the fruit it produces. There must be some unplanned and unstructured time in your life, where you can do whatever you feel like doing. During that time there should be a period of cessation from your usual activities. This pause in the daily grind is vital to allowing growth, healing, and recovery. It is similar in practice to the Israelites allowing their fields to rest every seven years. During this time the soil would rest to prevent overfarming the land and depletion of its natural resources. A key point to notice is that while resting the fields still had activity and growth. The gift of cessation does not require you to join a monastery, go on a silent retreat, or sit for hours staring at a blade of grass. It requires you only to open yourself to receive. The gift of cessation stops the bleeding in your life. It heals the slow leak draining your energy. Cessation is the restoration of you. We each need some unoccupied time every week to let the fertile ground of our heart and mind regenerate and replenish. What natural resources within you are being depleted by your lack of rest?

What if the key to the results you desire is not in doing more but in doing nothing on purpose? Sometimes the greatest power move you can make is doing nothing intentionally. When I say "intentionally," I mean doing it with a premeditated goal in mind. Now you may be thinking that if you are doing nothing, well, what exactly is there to premeditate? Let's start by redefining *nothing*. Doing nothing is not the same as no activity. How many times has someone called to ask what you're doing, and you reply, "Oh, nothing." Most of us do nothing accidentally all the time. Our nothing boils down to time spent doing activities with a hard-to-define outcome. When you watch a movie or TV show, you don't know how it will move you or affect your thinking. We call it doing nothing, but everything that affects our moods, emotions, energy, and strength is having a profound effect on who we become and the life we enjoy.

Could it be that failing to appropriate goals to our rest has led to a culture that cannot operate to its full potential because we've omitted one of our greatest resources? We have forgotten the power in doing nothing on purpose. We have neglected the gifts of sacred rest. The word in Hebrew that best describes this practice of sacred rest is *Shabbat*. It means rest or cessation of usual activity. It is time set aside on purpose to reflect on God and life.[1] Rigorous depleting activity is avoided in exchange for those activities that renew the mind, body, and spirit. It's a time to contemplate the spiritual, cherish loved ones, and enjoy the blessings in your life. It's doing nothing on purpose and choosing to be still despite much to do. Learning how to do nothing is necessary for thriving in an overwhelming life.

Does your rest have a purpose? Are you resting to renew? Do you need rest to release your creative flow? Does your rest have the purpose of spiritual revival? Has your rest drawn you closer to the people you love?

Intentional rest should make you a better person to be around. It should leave you feeling full and ready to pour into the lives of those around you. Purposeful rest leaves behind a residue of joy, and it ushers in the fruit of love, peace, kindness, and gentleness. It unlocks the revelations of heaven and releases creativity from the Creator to the created. It's the mystery behind the miraculous, the wind behind a presumed impossible flight.

Many religions see rest as vital to life and observe a Sabbath day, whether it's a Friday, Saturday, or Sunday. Now our weekends are as busy and stress-filled as any other day of the week. It's time to bring back Sunday. It's time to embrace your need for rest. Set apart time when you are excused from work and can devote yourself to pleasure and healing. I dare you to declare one day a week as Sacred Rest Day. Don't clean the house. Don't mow the lawn. Don't spend hours at the baseball field. Don't catch up on office work. Don't do the laundry. Don't glue yourself to a TV or computer. Savor the pleasures of cessation. Eat a great meal. Make love to your spouse. Play in the yard. Sip hot tea. Linger in a bath. Inhale fresh air. Love yourself.

Much of our doing is future-focused. We do to advance our careers. We do to have better bank accounts. We do so we can accomplish our goals and plans. All our doing pulls us out of the present. When we are living for the future instead of enjoying the present moment, it makes savoring life challenging. The gift of cessation awakens you to the present.

Ephesians 5:14–16 says: "Awake, you who sleep, arise from the dead, and Christ will give you light. See then that you walk circumspectly, not as fools but as wise, redeeming the time, because the days are evil" (NKJV). Living life future-oriented is like being asleep, or dead to the present. During your times of rest, your eyes will be opened. You will be able to see the light and love around you. Your times of endless activity will be redeemed with intentional rest. As you awake to what is meaningful, you will look at the people in your life with more appreciation. Awakening to the present is reinforced by every experience, every touch, every emotion, every conversation. When you stop doing, you become a noticer of life and can appreciate all it has to offer. The gift of cessation reminds you to treasure the sweetness of a smile, the brilliance of a firefly in the summer night, the gentle touch of a cool breeze, or the smell of warm cinnamon buns in the oven. It makes you thankful to be alive and awakens you to the present.

When *Nothing* Is the Answer

Don't expect doing nothing to feel easy at first. Resisting the need to hustle and bustle takes willpower. Often we spend ample energy on activities that will not reap the fruit we desire. Look at some situation in your life where you are doing all you know to do but not seeing the results you desire. Maybe it's time you cease pushing against a closed door, take a moment to step away, and do nothing. Let that problem, difficulty, or concern sit untouched while you regroup, so that the next time you approach it you will have a fresh perspective. This is easier said than done. It takes a mountain-moving, prayer-circling, water-walking mentality to determine the best thing you can do in a situation may be to do nothing. Below are some times it may be beneficial to do nothing while you await an answer that can be found in the gift of cessation.

> **Do nothing when you're burned out.** Isaiah 40:31 states, "But those who wait on the LORD shall renew *their* strength; they shall mount up with wings like eagles, they shall run and not be

weary, they shall walk and not faint" (NKJV). If you feel drained in more than three of the seven types of rest, you are experiencing burnout. Fatigue in the mind, body, or spirit affects every other area in your life. The best next step is not trying to fix yourself by adding more activities to your already packed schedule. The best next step is rest and lots of it. Slow down the pace of your life until you gain the energy to press on. In the waiting and ceasing, your strength will be renewed.

Do nothing when you're upset. Emotion can lead you astray. Anger distorts your perception and results in an inappropriate response to a situation. When you wait until the heat settles down, you will perceive the surrounding events with clarity. "Be quick to hear, slow to speak, slow to anger; for the anger of man does not produce the righteousness of God" (James 1:19–20 ESV). Anger can produce only more hurt and more pain. Be willing to cease until your anger abates, then when you do reply, your words will have the power to mend and repair.

Do nothing when your creativity wanes. Ideas and innovative thoughts bloom in a content spirit and a hushed mind. How many times have you participated in a brainstorming session to come up dry, only to have your mind flooded with creative thoughts after you've spent some time away from the meeting? Doing nothing removes the responsibility of creativity and allows it to happen naturally. In the beginning, God's spirit hovered over the waters. "All things were made through him, and without him was not any thing made that was made" (John 1:3 ESV). His spirit continues to hover, listening for what you will create.

Do nothing when you're afraid. Fear can cause you to accept a truth that does not exist. It can lead you down a false path and result in poor choices. When you are afraid, step away for a time. Focus on what you know to be true rather than what you think or imagine. Don't go back. Don't push forward. Stay put for a moment and analyze the reality of the present. Hear the still small voice whispering, "For I am the LORD your God who takes hold of your right hand and says to you, Do not fear; I will help you" (Isa. 41:13 NIV).

Do nothing when you're anxious. Anxiety changes us on the inside. Our heart rate increases, our breathing comes in quick pants, and our body tenses in response to the impending danger. The danger causing most of our anxieties is from the debris of our hurry-up lives. Doing nothing during times of debilitating anxiety will allow peace to sweep through, each wave clearing out some of the clutter. It's an opportunity to cast your cares and fix your thoughts on God's love for you (see 1 Pet. 5:7). Why exhaust yourself by running from the dangers you can defeat with rest and loving care?

Chapter 20

The Gift of Art

Where are you right now as you read these words? You may be reclining on your couch at home, sitting at a desk in an office, or lounging in your bed. What's around you? Who's with you? Is there any beauty to behold? Some of you may reply, "Nope, nothing beautiful about my office." Or, some of you may say, "Yes, I'm surrounded by beauty." Others may counter with the cliché "Beauty is in the eye of the beholder."

Since I can't peek into your life, let me tell you where I am and what I see in my room. I am sitting at my writing desk. Two laptops and an extra monitor occupy the small desk surface. Beside them sits a brown leather-bound Bible, a pink journal, and notepad. To my left stands a floor lamp with shelving space. On the shelves are small reminders of words that shape my life like faith, family, love, hope, and friends. A worship song just finished playing on YouTube. It's quiet now with the exception of the faint noise of traffic coming from the nearby street. May I share the beauty I see with you? I see beauty in the contrasts. My hopes recorded in my pink journal lying against the formality of my brown Bible. I see beauty in the words surrounding me. Each holds out a promise of what is available to me when my work today is done. I see beauty in the melody of a heartfelt song. But enough about me; let's take a look at the beauty you see.

We are connoisseurs of beauty. This is easily witnessed in how we respond to nature. Have you ever heard anyone say, "That was an ugly sunset"? Probably not, but I bet you've heard the words "That was a beautiful sunset!" many times. I love the beauty of God's creation. Just take a look around you. Beauty can be found anywhere. God's artistic side can be seen in the snow-covered peaks of majestic mountains, cascading waterfalls, the rich hues of blooming flowers, and the vastness of the heavens. Each declares the glory of God and shows His handiwork (see Ps. 19:1). He not only creates beauty out of nothing, but also designed the very materials out of which all things are made (see Rev. 4:11). He masterfully uses colors, form, and textures to reveal life. Like visitors at a holy art exhibit, we must praise the artist for the beauty of His work.

God loves not only to create beauty; He loves to share beauty. He shared beauty with Adam by inviting him into the creative process and allowing him to name every living creature. Adam was allowed to use the materials he had before him—words and vocabulary—to create. God did not hesitate in this proposition. He did not preface it with, "It's OK, Adam, if you get writer's block." Or "You may not be talented enough for this task, but give it a try, Adam." No, He was confident of Adam's creative capacities. He knew art does not come from some unknown source or random inspiration. It comes from a deep inner well. It comes from deep calling to deep, drawing beauty to the surface. From the depths of our soul, we release the gift of our art.

The Old Testament is full of examples of God's love of beauty. In Exodus 25, He commissioned numerous forms of art to be made for the tabernacle including tapestry, metal moldings, clothing, furniture, and architecture. The Creator was sharing again the work of creation with humanity. Music and dance are also shown to be pleasing to God. Remember King David, the man who danced so hard he lost his pants? He was called a man after God's own heart. The Old Testament does not stop with just these material and musical offerings of art, but also shares many examples of poetry, including Psalms, Proverbs, Ecclesiastes, and Song of Solomon. All Scripture is given by inspiration of God, not just the retelling of the stories but the very way in which they are shared (see 2 Tim. 3:16).

Art was even how God provided for the healing and restoration of the Israelites in the wilderness. During that time, many were dying from poisonous snakebites. God had the people craft an image of a snake on a rod and instructed Moses to hold it up. When the people saw the image, they were healed. "And as Moses lifted up the serpent in the wilderness, even so must the Son of man be lifted up: That whosoever believeth in him should not perish, but have eternal life" (John 3:14–15 KJV). Even today, the symbol used to represent the medical profession is a serpent on a rod. Art has the ability to heal when it references the Healer.

The New Testament also includes examples of God's appreciation of art and beauty. Jesus was often praised for his ability as a skilled storyteller. His teachings are full of parables and fictional stories used to help bring new insight to old problems. He used the power of words to bring to life spiritual truths. For that matter, the Bible is considered one of the greatest influences on art in history. From the stained-glass windows at your local church to Michelangelo's *David*, we see the gift of art expressed.

Right about now you may be thinking, *But wait, I'm not an artist, a musician, a writer, or a poet. I don't do art.* Let me stop you right there and suggest something. You don't have to *do* art; you *are* art. Take this paradigm shift with me. What exactly is art? Art is the expression of human creative skill, typically in a visual form, appreciated primarily for its beauty or emotional power.[1] Art is humanity displayed for all to see. The gift of art releases you to share your portion of the big picture by using the materials life has given you. Your experiences become the color used to adorn your offerings, and your relationships become the textures in your story.

Some people wield in clay. They have experienced the stickiness of being in the pit and take the mud slung at them to mold something full of truth and honesty. Their art carries the power to come alongside others in the pit and let them know they are not alone. Some work in pastels. They have spent much of their time in the joys of life. They are the cheerleaders encouraging and uplifting others on their journey. Others create with oils. They have survived tight places in their life and slipped through to the other side. They use the canvas of trouble as their backdrop and paint a picture of hope for the future.

Notice each type of art I've mentioned results in a positive response in the one beholding it. It creates beauty to be appreciated. It does not create fear or doubt. The gift of art sifts the lovely out of the ugly. It calls forth the purpose from the pain. It carves out the faith from the worry. Art is more than just skill and talent. If that's all you bring, you'll leave us wanting. Art should express truth from your experiences. It should reveal the hidden beauty of being pressed on all sides. Life is hard to appreciate without the pressing. In the process, we learn the value of gratitude during the good times and mercy during the bad. Time passes between the pressing and the expressing. In the process of waiting, art is revealed.

"Art is a collaboration between God and the artist, and the less the artist does the better."[2]

ANDRÉ GIDE

Art and creativity flourish from your time spent in creative rest. Seek out beauty and spend time in its presence. Not analyzing it but simply enjoying it. As you become refreshed and energized, move from experiencing art to creating it. Your artistic expression can take many forms, including painting, drawing, crafting, sculpting, cooking, baking, photographing, writing, doing spoken word, and acting. These activities are not rest, but they arise from a place of rest. They are the gift of art birthed from your rest. When your soul is allowed room to expand and grow, the resulting creativity can be surprising, leading you to express God in a way uniquely specific to your life's journey. This world needs the gift of your art, full of truth and beauty.

Chapter 21

The Gift of Communication

The worn science textbook smelled of PB&J. Half its pages were forever merged by a sticky goo I hoped was jelly. My son and I assumed our study positions to review chapter 6 for his upcoming test. Fourth-grade science is full of discovery. Every bug, element, chemical process, and scientific theory laid out to marvel over. This week's test included a section on how different species communicate. The study guide included a web link titled "World's Weirdest: Honey Bee Dance Moves."[1] I don't know any kid who could pass up watching a video about the world's weirdest anything, so of course we had to watch.

The video showed how honey bees communicate with each other through dance. Their dance conveys information that helps them find food and survive. The guide went on to describe studies showing that if a bee is fatigued, its ability to dance is altered and it can miscommunicate information. That single burned-out bee can wreak havoc in the hive and can ultimately lead to the demise of all associated with it. The lack of rest affects every aspect of nature, from the large to the small.

Communication within your home and at your job is just as important. When your life is overwhelmed by stress and never-ending activity, you cannot process all of the incoming information around you. Most of us shut down. We resist talking and don't have the energy or the attention span to listen to another word. As our ability to communicate falters, so do our relationships and our family stability. Our lack of rest affects not only our communication with those in our lives but also our communication with God. His voice becomes a distant memory of when we had time to listen. The gift of communication restores your ability to listen to your body so you can become a better listener in other areas of your life.

Listening is one of the most important skills we can have. How well we listen has a major impact on the quality of our relationships, our job effectiveness, and our level of personal contentment. We often confuse listening with hearing. Hearing is one of our five senses. We can hear things without even trying. It is a physical process that happens automatically with no cooperation needed. Listening requires more from us. It requires focus, concentration, and a desire to receive what is being shared. Listening means paying attention not only to the words being spoken but also to the pitch, expression, volume, and tone of the one speaking. It means being aware of both verbal and nonverbal messages being offered. Our ability to listen well depends on how accurate we perceive and understand these messages.

Given we have two ears and only one mouth, you would think we'd be great listeners. The truth is most of us are not. Psychiatrist and researcher William Glasser suggests we remember only 20 percent of what we hear.[2] That means when you talk to your kids, spouse, or colleagues they may recall only a tiny fraction of the conversation. They are not benefitting from the whole message. Hopefully, the part that sticks is the important thing, but what if it's not? In contrast, when there is active discussion, we can retain more than 70 percent of the same conversation. This give-and-take in communication creates an experience. Experiences tap into your thoughts and emotions, which in turn find space in your memory. Good listeners experience more of life. By becoming a better listener, you'll learn more from your interactions with others, which will improve your communication skills and help you create successful relationships. Listening is a skill we can all benefit from improving.

Your Soul's Love Language

Rest quiets life so you can listen with your spirit. It removes the distractions. It pulls us close with both hands on our cheeks, and whispers, "I'm right here with you." Rest is your soul's love language. It communicates in a way your soul understands and mends the brokenness of the hurtful words of others. Contrary to the old saying, words can hurt. I know because I've been on the receiving and the hurling end of a word dagger. Recoiling when wounded, then lashing back. Ripping into those closest to me when the overwhelming became too much. Slashing up delicate emotions in pursuit of doing more, being more, and having more. When words become your weapon, practice silence. Rest will remind you to be gentle with your words, quick to listen, slow to speak, and slow to become angry (see James 1:19).

Transformational communication is a gift. It reaches into the deepest part of our understanding, bypassing the intellect and going straight to our spiritual core. It speaks to our heart without asking permission from our mind. Enjoying this gift requires us to be in position to receive. It is the opposite of the type of communication most of us practice. When we have a conversation with someone, long before they ever stop talking we start to think about what we are going to say in reply. We stop giving them our full attention because we are eager to share our story. When the one talking begins to notice our lack of interest in what they have to say, they will be less inclined to share with us in the future, or they may become offended and upset. As we discussed in part I, every story is important and desires being shared, but don't neglect the gift of communication in exchange for a fleeting taste of emotional and social rest. Unless this gift is ingested, it can't be digested and you miss much of the goodness inside of it.

Even your prayer life can suffer if you ignore the gift of communication. Prayer doesn't have to contain rhyming words and memorized Scriptures to be heard by God. God hears them all, the rushed prayer as you scramble to get everyone off in the morning, the hushed prayer in an ICU waiting room, and the crushed prayer beside a burial site. He not only hears; He is attentively listening (see Ps. 34:15). He is forever upholding His part of the communication equation. In our prayers asking for wisdom, guidance, hope, and comfort, we leave no time to hear a response. We pray without leaning in to listen. We speak to God without the benefit of listening for His reply. Frustration builds because we assume God does not care. But He does care and is constantly trying to communicate with us. How frustrating it must be to speak to someone who refuses to listen to you. It reminds me of a couple who came in to see me. The wife complained that her husband could not hear and wanted me to check his hearing. She was so upset because she said she always had to repeat things to him over and over again. Even with her constant chatter, he didn't do the things she was asking him to do. I picked up my tuning fork to check his hearing. I looked into his ear canal with my otoscope. I even whispered from across the room in the softest voice I could. His hearing was excellent. I looked at this gentleman and asked: "What's going on with your hearing?" He replied, "There is nothing wrong with my hearing, Doc. I hear every word out of her mouth. I choose not to listen." How sad!

Even more sad is the fact that sometimes we choose not to listen to God. We pray. He listens. He speaks. We keep right on talking. We move on with our day, hoping He will answer. The answers keep coming in the form of wisdom, revelation, and knowledge spoken to ears numb from constant noise. We fear He does not care, that we are not deserving of His attention, or that we are not worthy of His love. Our fears are left untouched by His comfort because of our restless hearts.

Resting in God requires the gift of communication. It means stopping our endless activity to spend time talking and listening to God. The rest of God flows from this interaction. In resting, we unwrap this gift. In listening, we receive. We listen to obtain information about the plans God has for us (see Jer. 29:11). We listen to be encouraged in our inner self (see Eph. 3:16). We listen to learn who we are (see Gen. 32:28). We listen to hear the sound of joy coming in the morning (see Ps. 30:5). We listen to hear God sending help in our time of need (see 2 Sam. 5:24). We listen to enjoy the sound of Him singing over us (see Zeph. 3:17). And as we listen, we learn to dance again to the unforced rhythm of grace (see Matt. 11:28–30).

The lyrics of one of my favorite worship songs "The More I Seek You," state: "I want to sit at your feet. Drink from the cup in your hand. Lay back against you and breathe, feel your heart beat. This love is so deep, it's more than I can stand. I melt in your peace, it's overwhelming."[3] This is the overwhelming feeling we crave. To be overwhelmed by peace, joy, and contentment. To have margin in our lives and enough room to dance to the rhythm of rest. To be able to savor the holy and recline in its embrace. To lean upon the chest of God and hear His heart in all things. *Shhh.* Let us listen and see what He is saying now.

Chapter 22

The Gift of Productivity

Every new adventure in life begins with a journey of courage, nerves, joy, and excitement. This was the journey I had getting my medical degree. It was also the journey I found when I got married and when I became a parent. Each of these life events brims with new things to learn and new responsibilities. Each is a branch off the withering tree that had become my burned-out life. I was convinced every woman knew the secret to holding it all together but no one was willing to share it with me. Every New Year I would search for the latest greatest information on productivity, efficiency, multitasking, and anything else that would help me get the job done. That job, in my mind, was being a woman who could do it all and do it well without having a nervous breakdown. I would love to say that I succeeded at accomplishing that goal, but the reality is I failed miserably at being Superwoman and had to hang up my cape. During those first few years, the three greatest joys of my life all collided. It was a train wreck waiting to happen. Career, marriage, and parenthood were like three boulders heaped upon my weak frame. I was being crushed by the life I had built. I was producing lots of good fruit, but I didn't have a moment left in my day to taste and see what I was producing. Productivity is not simply getting things done. Productivity is getting things done that matter and seeing good fruits growing in your life. You can be busy and still lack productivity.

"It's not so much how busy you are, but why you are busy. The bee is praised. The mosquito is swatted."[1]

MARY O'CONNOR

Is your productivity producing the good fruit you desire? Are you a purpose-driven bee or a pesky mosquito? Both are busy, but the difference is the results of their busyness. The bee is perceived as more valuable than the mosquito because of the fruit it produces. The bee pollinates flowers and makes honey, both of which are things we find appealing to our senses. The mosquito, on the other hand, flies around sucking our blood, leaving us with itchy red bumps. One is fruitful, the other annoying. Is your busyness producing things that are lovely and sweet or has your overwhelming life become a painful annoyance?

The thought of taking time to rest is counterintuitive for most of us. The very idea of rest leading to productivity is at odds with current work culture. Since Genesis, we have been encouraged to be fruitful. This fruitfulness operates on the principle of seed time and harvest, which is a concept shown throughout the entire Bible beginning in Genesis 8:22 all the way to Revelation 14:4. However, fruitfulness is beneficial only if it produces good fruit. The goal cannot simply be to produce good fruit, but also for that fruit to remain (see John 15:16). We want the good fruit in our life to be available when we are ready to taste it. Productivity is what makes fruit last. It's what keeps the fruit in our lives thriving and growing so that we do not extinguish their supply. Productivity is how we prevent the fruit from spoiling before we have the opportunity to enjoy it.

What benefit is there to marriage if you never find time to share life and love? What benefit is there to parenting if you do not get to know your kids intimately? Presence does not equate to productivity. If you feel detached from those you care most about, there is something wrong with the fruit being produced. Bitterness, resentment, anger, fear, insecurity, exhaustion, and hopelessness are some of the rotten fruit we find when our productivity shifts from bee to mosquito. Busyness can be a very effective way to avoid dealing with feelings we are not ready to address. Rest is how we process. In rest, we find the grace and mercy to confront the issues in our life. It is impossible to produce at your highest level in the important areas in your life without allowing time for rest. Sometimes the most important thing in a day is the sacred rest you take in between your times of doing and existing.

Abiding Rest

In the Gospel of John chapter 15, Jesus teaches how abiding in Him leads to greater productivity. According to *Merriam-Webster*'s online dictionary, *abide* means "to remain stable or fixed in a state" or "to continue in a place."[2] As we abide, we rest and we learn how to dwell in a place of rest. Everything else comes from that place. Abiding rest is when you remain stable in your place of rest. Rest becomes the ground from which all your good fruit is produced, and you can see Jesus in it all. He connects you to the sustaining power of God's grace, and He reminds you to go deeper into rest. This rest equips you for every good work. The deeper you go, the more productive you become.

Abiding is also defined as having to wait or to accept without obligation. It means learning to wait without becoming restless, and it's the ability to accept the process of rest without obligation. Abiding rest brings you face-to-face with your limitations and God's "all things are possible."[3] It challenges you to see waiting as an invitation to rest and trust. It is a self-reinforcing lesson in rest. Can you rest in the waiting? Can you differentiate a pause from an end? Let's take a look at how this process of abiding rest leads to the gift of productivity.

We are connected by God's spirit to Jesus, who is the vine, and God is the gardener overseeing the vine (see John 15:1). Enemies may try to trample the vineyard (see Jer. 12:10–11). These enemies come in the form of people who attempt to manipulate your emotions to force you to say yes when you need to say no, or in the form of a to-do list with more than you could possibly do in twenty-four hours. God lovingly tends to the vine and carefully looks for fruit (see Isa. 5:1–7). He has expectations of what the vine can produce when nurtured properly.[4]

We are branches growing from the abiding rest of God. Each branch is capable of more than we could ever imagine. When He sees us bearing good fruit He prunes us, so that we may bear more fruit (see John 15:2). Every place it seems like God is taking something away will ultimately become a place of growth. Yes, there will be fruit even after whatever thought of loss just entered your mind. God's purpose is loving, but the trimming still hurts in the moment. Abiding rest reminds us to trust in His goodness even when goodness is not what we are experiencing at the time.

During the pruning, you must cling closer to the vine. As you abide in Jesus, He abides in you. A branch cannot bear fruit by itself, unless it abides in the vine, and neither can you, unless you abide in Him (see John 15:4–5). You cannot produce the strength you need on your own. You can receive it only from the vine. This reveals the greatness of God's tender care, as we contribute nothing to the vine but from it draw all we need to live fully. It supplies everything we need for life and godliness (see 2 Pet. 1:3). It flows from the divine into the natural. You cannot be self-sufficient if you want to produce good fruit in your life. Rather, you need to be one who is always receiving from the overflow of heaven through the process of abiding rest.

When we refuse to abide and rest, we become a branch that withers and is burned (see John 15:6). We burn out and live a fruitless life. Our hope and joy are dried up by our lack of attention to our physical, spiritual, emotional, mental, social, sensory, and creative needs. Such a life ends in despair, although when viewed from the outside, it may appear to be productive and successful. Our culture desperately needs to redefine success. In her book *Thrive*, Arianna Huffington described success as a life of well-being, wisdom, and wonder—three things that can be found only when we take time to tap into sacred rest.[5]

We often confuse activity with productivity. If you spend your day busy on numerous tasks, you can mistakenly assume all your work was necessary and useful. Have you ever had a day packed from sunrise to sunset with activity, but when you sit down at the end of the day you feel like you didn't get anything accomplished? The next time you're sitting at your desk plowing through stacks of papers or you're home sorting through piles of laundry for hours on end with no break, consider if what you're producing is the fruit you desire for that day. Checking off boxes on your to-do list can give you a sense of accomplishment and can mistakenly lead you to believe you have mastered productivity. I pray you want more out of your days than a clean desk and folded clothes.

Try checking off these to-dos:

____ Spend ten minutes of face-to-face time with each child having your undivided attention.

____ Look into the eyes of your spouse until everything in you wants to dive in for a deep kiss.

____ Call one friend you adore but you never have time to chat with and ask about her day.

____ Walk, run, skip, dance, or move in any way you desire for fifteen minutes just because you can. Even those who are allergic to exercise can find something fun to do with their bodies.

____ De-stress in your mind and body with stretching poses while you pray or meditate on a favorite Scripture.

____ Got toddlers? Grab a few crayons and color together.

____ Got teens? Grab a coffee or smoothie together and discuss anything they want to talk about.

____ Got aging parents? Volunteer to go with them to their next doctor's appointment and treat them to a lunch date afterward.

We taste life by taking small bites out of the big themes: family, love, career, truth, relationships, health, desire, happiness, freedom, and purpose. The more bites you enjoy, the sweeter your life will be. When you make time for rest, you make time to taste and see the fruit you are producing. What will you check off your to-do list today?

Chapter 23

The Gift of Choice

Every day you make choices about how to spend your time, your energy, your attention, and your resources. Some of these choices will be decisions you make after contemplation and prayerful consideration. Most of your choices will be an automatic response to situations, ideas, assumptions, or circumstances that occur during the day. How many times have you set a goal to exercise or eat better, but when you've planned to work out or cook you've got other more pressing matters vying for your time? Every yes and every no is a choice, and these choices affect your future. Your choices do not operate in a vacuum. They affect you, as well as everyone and everything attached to you. Some of your choices may fall like a pebble in a lake, creating a ripple effect and touching what's near and dear to you. Or your choices may fall like a rock down a snow-covered mountain, picking up speed and power as they bring an avalanche of trouble with them.

Most of the choices you make will have a profound impact on your well-being. A single bad choice could balloon into a series of bad circumstances, causing damage to every area of your life. Eating healthy foods and being physically active will help prevent chronic disease and illness. A lack of rest or working while physically exhausted can impair your judgment, leading to accidents and injury. Your emotional health is affected by how you respond to mental pressures. Reducing stress in your life can help prevent a depressed and anxious mind. Your social health is determined by the choices you make for or against building relationships. Cherishing those you love builds connections that can endure through both good and hard times. Spending time enjoying God and His creation will fortify your spiritual health, which in turn influences your attitude and how you respond to the choices presented to you.

Power to Choose Better

Your life and your enjoyment of it are the sum of the choices you make. Good choices increase joy and blessings in your life, while poor choices increase worry, disease, and fear. It's important to be mindful of the choices you make and to be careful not to abuse the gift of choice. I once stood in front of a patient with numerous health problems, many of which were related to her poor diet and lack of self-care. I could not understand why she often returned to her appointments unhealthier than the time before. One day she confided, "I feel powerless to choose better." You always have the gift of choice, but the power to choose better is a matter of the heart.

The power to choose better begins with rest. Rest reminds you that you are not the creator of power, but the recipient. Rest is a restorer of the breach. It traverses the gap between our weakness and God's enabling power. In rest, you welcome God into the process, and you admit you cannot choose better on your own. When you open yourself to God, you also open yourself to experiencing His spirit as helper, comforter, advocate, intercessor, counselor, strengthener, and standby (see John 16:7). You may fear making choices when you are stressed because you fear the outcome of the decisions made when you are in a vulnerable state. During these times it is even more important to rest. This is when you need God's spirit to guide your choices. Some decisions keep you weak, and some have the ability to restore your strength. Rest is always a good decision for a tired body and a weakened spirit.

When you spend the best of your energy pursuing power, pleasure, wealth, significance, happiness, acceptance, praise, or positions, you choose to believe the lie that these things can bring you joy, security, peace, and satisfaction. These lies are attitudes, belief systems, and faulty expectations that are not supported by Scripture. Rest dares you to replace lies with truth. You get to choose to either believe the lies or walk in the truth. Don't worry; it's OK if you stumble along the way. I've tripped many times and fallen back into believing these lies. The good news is no matter how many times we fall, we have the choice to get back up (see Prov. 24:16).

In my book *Set Free to Live Free: Breaking Through the 7 Lies Women Tell Themselves*, I confront the devastating lies that have led many to make poor choices because of flawed beliefs about God, their self-worth, and the inherent potential in their life.[1] Beliefs you can find time to conquer only when you allow rest to be your guide to truth.

The ability to rest boils down to the condition of your heart. Can you trust God to supply while you rest? If you give up time for intentional rest, will you still be able to do, have, be, and own all that you desire? Rest is a heart choice. Life and death. Blessings and cursing are daily set before you. You can choose to stay bound by your day planner and calendar, or you can declare freedom from the bondage of your hectic schedules. Every heart needs rest. You rest your heart when you decontaminate the clogged vessels of your spirit by regularly choosing your personal best option over a quick option with fleeting benefits. When you search your heart for what really matters, your heart can rest in the knowledge it is well with your soul.

Make a Heart Choice:

- Live in the present or live for the future.
- Live life on purpose or wander through your life haphazardly.
- Believe in the power of hope or drown in the feeling of hopelessness.
- Receive help when needed or become overwhelmed by responsibilities.
- Adapt to change or push yourself to the breaking point.
- Forgive or allow hate and resentment to consume you.
- Love with an open heart or stay isolated behind your walls.
- Grow in faith or stay rooted in fear.
- Release the pain of the past or hold on to your wounds.
- Embrace the promise of tomorrow or relent to anxiety about the unknowns.
- Accept the gifts of rest or cling to the ashes of your burned-out life.

Which heart choices do you need to make to live a well-rested life?

Chapter 24

The Gift of Faith

We began this journey together with me supine on my hardwood floor. Ten years ago I found myself depleted, empty, and in a compromised position because of my lack of rest. I was an emotional, physical, and spiritual mess. I had a busy medical practice and two beautiful toddler boys, and I was married to a man I adore. On the surface, my life looked Pinterest perfect, but on the inside I was unraveling under the pressures of trying to hold it all together in my own strength. I found that the blessings in a woman's life are often the greatest stressors too. Although I was open to God's help, I had neglected taking the needed steps to invite Him into my situation. I wasn't willing to slow down long enough for faith to arise. I've found even the gifts of God come with great responsibility and pressures. I didn't have enough faith to handle another gift without feeling overwhelmed. My strength ran out, and I found myself desperate for help. The gift of faith was the lifeline pulling me back to a life I enjoy. This is where GRACE (**G**od's **R**esurrecting power **A**ctively **C**hanging and **E**mpowering my life) found me. It led me to a place of rest I did not realize was available.

Finding your GRACE place is an invitation to determine what areas of your life need the resurrecting power of God to come in and make a change for the better. It's an opportunity to discover the gift of faith by first receiving the gift of rest. It isn't an excuse for not taking action, but a prayerful plan on what will lead you to the abundant life Jesus offers in John 10:10. It forces you to evaluate what you are pursuing and what's pursuing you. We chase all the pieces of our day, from our to-do list to dinner, without taking the needed time for the whole, for self-care and soul-care. We get a lot of things done at the expense of ourselves. The gift of faith is how you find your way back to discover your life's splendor. It takes you on a journey to finding your GRACE place and reclaiming your life.

One of my favorite books is *Hinds' Feet on High Places*.[1] It begins by discussing the life of the main character, Much-Afraid. It's a name given to her because of her past of fear, shame, and regret. The Good Shepherd extends to her an invitation to go on a journey to find her new name, her redeemed name. This is similar to the process each of us must go through. We start unable to recognize who we are and how we got here. We then take faith steps that either bring us closer to the life we desire or lead us further away. And if we are fortunate, our steps will take us on a journey that will redeem every loss, every missed opportunity, and every disappointment. Let's take a look at some of the places you will encounter as you unwrap the gift of faith.

Journey to Your GRACE Place

The Secret Place. Your faith journey begins in the secret place. It is available to all, but many will never find it. You must search it out in the wilderness of discontentment, disappointment, and despair. There will be some difficult terrain to overcome. There are hills you must climb and some valleys you will travel through on your journey. It is mandatory that you travel light. There is no room for bitterness, anger, envy, pride, unforgiveness, fear, rebellion, or impure motives in your backpack.

The secret place is a holy place close to God. It is the place where His presence becomes as real to you as the person sitting beside you. It is a place of intimacy, trust, love, and continuous fellowship with the Lord. It is a place He wants you not only to find but ultimately to dwell in. It is the sanctuary of the well rested. The place you kick off your shoes to step on holy ground. He wants you to get so comfortable in this place that you see it as the place where you belong, the place where you abide.

What is the greatest obstacle keeping you from entering into the secret place? What tries to edge God out of your life?

The Tomb. This is my least favorite part of the journey because it's uncomfortable. It's the stuff we don't want to talk about but also the stuff that tends to have the greatest impact on our lives. Every one of us has experienced loss. I imagine the types of losses represented by those reading this book include everything from the loss of a parent or a child, to the loss of a job or a marriage. Whatever the loss, the pain is real, and it's in those places of our woundedness we tend to overcompensate the most for fear of being hurt again. For example, if you've lost a job or position in the past, you will be more likely to be a workaholic because your defense mechanisms will say, "If I do this, then this won't happen." It's important to recognize those places where your tears fell because it's those same tears God uses to soften the hard ground of our soul. And it's here that we begin to understand God's resurrecting power.

By definition, resurrection is the act of returning life. God's resurrecting power works best in those places of our life that seem hopeless and impossible. There isn't one dry place in your life that God does not have the ability to speak life back into. Joy can be resurrected, peace can be resurrected, hope can be resurrected, and faith can be resurrected. The resurrecting power of God is strong enough to redeem your past. It is powerful enough to conquer life's problems. It is potent enough to change your behavior. It is effective and competent in its ability to renew your mind. It is the same power that raised Christ from the dead and seated Him at the right hand of the God (see Eph. 1:20). That same power is available to you.

So let's make this practical: If your spouse has become more like a roommate, passion needs a resurrection in your relationship. If your prayer time has turned into your Facebook time, spiritual discipline needs resurrecting. If your kids feel more like a burden than a blessing, you need a resurrection of gratitude in your attitude. When you've got God's resurrection power actively working within your life, you can rest in the assurance that no matter how dark a situation may be, God can turn it around. You cannot change something you will not confront, so let's confront those places that need God's resurrecting power. What areas or situations in your life do you feel powerless to change?

The River of Release. I wish I could say change is easy and you can snap your fingers and find yourself well rested and living the good life. It's not. You have to let go of some things so you can enjoy others. You have to be an active participant in the process. Some choices may begin with a recommendation from your doctor. Some choices may start with poor outcomes you want to improve. Others may begin with a suggestion from a trusted friend. With each choice, you pick up something and release something. Rest flows from this release. Many of us need to release our worries and anxious thoughts. Or you may need to release fear or doubt. You may need to release a dream that no longer fits or a plan that you never inquired of God about. There is no judgment on what you need to release. The point is to stay on the journey with God. The wonderful thing about the river of release is it sweeps you right into the third stop. Because at this point you are ready to see the active changes only God can provide.

The Place of Mending. Jeremiah 18:3–4 states, "Then I went down to the potter's house, and there he was, making something at the wheel. And the vessel that he made of clay was marred in the hand of the potter; so he made it again into another vessel, as it seemed good to the potter to make" (NKJV).

Clay is not easy to work with. A couple of years ago my son came home from school with something white and sticky all over his clothes. I asked him what this was and he replied, "Sorry, Mom, my clay was too wet." His class was attempting to make special cups as a surprise for Mother's Day, but someone had put too much water in the clay mixture. Instead of a firm, sturdy, pliable clay that could be molded, what they had to work with was a sticky, gooey, weak mixture that refused to conform to the desired shapes.

Before clay can be put upon the wheel, it has to be properly prepared. It has to be supple enough to adapt to change yet secure enough to not collapse under pressure. We are like clay. Before God can begin changing us, some preparations have to happen. This is where the rebuilding and renewing of the mind occur. In the place of mending, we have to patch up some of the wounds of our past and get rid of some lies we've believed and exchange them for God's truth. This is where the physician within me gets so excited. Broken cisterns hold no water (see Jer. 2:13). They are incapable of staying filled with the living water of joy, contentment, peace, and love. It's a beautiful moment when someone realizes they don't have to stay broken. What lies have you believed? What truth from God's word can you use to mend the broken places?

The Well. Once taken off the potter's wheel, you are not sent off alone to live your life. The Potter deposits a part of Himself inside of you. He fills you with the living water of His spirit so you can pour out His love and truth into the lives of others. It is not something that you can do on your own. It's an empowerment from Him to do what you cannot do alone.

This is where many of us need to stay awhile, pull up a chair, grab a cup of coffee or a glass of sweet tea. The well is our place of filling, restoration, and revival. We need to remain at the well until our spiritual tanks are replenished. We need to stay put until our love, peace, joy, kindness, and goodness tanks overflow. It's from this place that we can do our best work. It's from this place that we can go into our respective homes, offices, and communities energized and excited. It's from this place you can leave from a mentally stressful day of pouring into the lives of others and still have something left to pour into your family. You have to visit the well often. It's the place to run to when you feel like running away from it all. It's where you can come empty to pour out life's hurts and receive God's healing love.[2] It's a mandatory stop to feel well rested, and it's the only way to get to physical and emotional wellness. It's the place you have to remember to return to when you feel overwhelmed, to ask, "Lord, help me see where my life is getting out of balance and give me GRACE for the necessary changes."

The GRACE Place. As you learn to trust God on this journey, you will find it easier to rest. Rest is an act of seeking, and "He is a rewarder of those who diligently seek Him" (Heb. 11:6 NKJV). This is not an act of working to give God your best, but to trust in His desire to give you His best. Faith consists not in doing more but receiving more. It's accepting the gifts with outstretched arms. The gifts of rest do not cease being gifts because you choose not to receive.

Rest is a living testimony of your faith. It is demonstrated when you respond to God's principles and promises regardless of how things currently appear. It's trusting Him for what you cannot see with your eyes, but which you know He has the ability to provide. The ultimate purpose of sacred rest is for you to enjoy God, enjoy people, and enjoy your life's splendor. Sacred rest is worth the journey into your best life. It is a chance for your faith to be strengthened as you learn how to lean on Him and how to accomplish more even when physically doing less. It's becoming reacquainted with the life you've created and how you can enjoy it to the fullest. May the gift of faith be the compass leading you to your life's splendor: hidden beauty, captivating uniqueness, divine glory, radiant light, and brilliant distinctions. Once this splendor is revealed, you will no longer feel overwhelmed by life, but overcome with gratitude for your life and the many opportunities welcoming you to live fully, love boldly, and rest intentionally.

PART III

THE PROMISES
OF REST

"Standing on the promises I shall not fall,
List'ning every moment to the Spirit's call.
Resting in my Savior as my All in all,
Standing on the promises of God."

RUSSELL K. CARTER, "STANDING
ON THE PROMISES"

Chapter 25

I Choose My Best Life

On my way home this evening I listened to some of my favorite music and allowed the melody to create a new song within my heart. My soul reclined. My hopes, dreams, failures, and successes were all brought together within the rhythm of rest. I turned off the music as I sat in the garage a few extra minutes. The kids were inside doing homework, and my husband hadn't arrived yet. For just a thimble of time, I sat in the silence of my car, allowing my mind to defuse and decontaminate. I never again want to bring the toxins of work life into the sanctuary of my home. I've made this a key part of my personal rest strategy. My home and my life are far from perfect, but they are worth protecting from unrest. A coworker with a bad attitude, the person who cut me off in traffic, the neighbor with a disapproving look toward my lawn—none of them are things I want to hold on to. None of them are worthy of permanent room in my mind, so one by one I discarded each thought. I cleared my head space so I could pinpoint my thoughts on the people and things I value. My husband will not become my dumping ground for today's disappointments. My kids will not be my venting wall. My family will reap the rewards of my head and heart pointing in the same direction. As my boot-clad feet hit the garage floor, I leaned into the sounds of life inside my home. Life can be noisy, but even in the reverberations, God is always softly speaking.

The evening concluded with takeout from our favorite Chinese restaurant, free from working-mom guilt over giving my family food from a little white box. I've laid down the maternal burden of unrealistic expectations. Every meal does not have to be home cooked for me to be a good mother. A nourishing meal, even one prepared by the hands of others, was a welcome addition to the laughter and conversation with my family around the dinner table.

My boys headed to bed a few hours later, and I found myself alone for the first time that evening with my husband. I snuggled up beside him on the sofa and welcomed his hand caressing my back. My desire for intimacy had been nonexistent for years, and it created a wedge in our marriage. Rest taught me how to love and how to be loved. I now look forward to these times of closeness and have found it to be an important part of a well-rested life. Later that night as I lay in bed listening to the sound of his breathing, I joined him and breathed a reverential thank-you into the heavens for the beauty arising from the ashes of my life. I isolated the tense muscles in my legs and stretched them into quiet resolve. I cleared my mind of my unfinished to-do list and unresolved conversations. There was no sense engaging in tomorrow's work. That night I chose rest.

* * *

I wish I could say every day flows this well. Like you, my life is not all rainbows and sunshine. Some days are easier than others. But every day I make a choice to rest, and it has transformed me. Rest has become my go-to source for strength, creativity, productivity, peace, joy, hope, and contentment. I've found it to be the best-kept secret in medicine.

In 2008, a large study asked people how they viewed their lives.[1] This study showed a staggering 55 percent deemed their lives as difficult or struggling. If you are sitting in an airport reading this book or in a coffee shop sipping a frappé look around. Over half the people in the room with you are miserable. Marriages are failing. Suicide is on the rise. We are turning to anything that gives us a sense of freedom. Many have come to the belief that this is as good as it gets. But that is not everyone's final answer. It is certainly not mine. I don't believe it's yours.

Yes, I have days when life deals me a disappointing hand. And there are times when my diet is not always the best, I skip exercise, I worry unnecessarily, and I fail to give my family the attention they deserve. But I refuse to let those times define me. They are simply moments in a busy life when I fail to choose what is best for me. They are times when I need to be reminded how my choices affect my outcome and why rest is required to live well. It's a principle I share with my patients and all those I love because life's too short to sit by and let it slip away untouched.

You alone can choose your best life. You have to decide to make rest a priority. Choose to find times for physical rest, mental rest, emotional rest, spiritual rest, social rest, sensory rest, and creative rest. I have found these seven types of rest to be essential in my life and the lives of thousands of others. Your ability to identify which types of rest you are missing and correct your rest deficit is the key to enjoying the gifts and promises of rest.

The Promises of Rest

Renew Your Energy

Your body needs both active and passive forms of physical rest: active rest to remove the tension you build as you work hard, and passive rest in the form of quality sleep to replenish your energy and heal your body. Downtime is where you recharge and prepare for another day. As you unplug from electronics and continuous sensory input, you reap the benefits of sensory rest. You cannot have an energized life without downtime, and plenty of it. Each hiatus from your normal depleting activities renews your energy by letting you tap into the source of all strength and vitality through the gifts of cessation, freedom, and exchange.

Restore Your Sanity

Restoring your sanity is harder than it sounds because it requires you to trust yourself, to love yourself, and to be patient with yourself. It requires you to honor the boundaries of your well-rested life. As you accept your need for mental and emotional rest, you create calm within the chaos through nonjudgmental decluttering. You can see the debris of your thought life without allowing it to change how you view who you are. Most of us have no clue how to do this, and we lose control of our head space, opening it up to whatever wants to take up residence there. Rest reminds us to use the gifts of boundaries, reflection, acceptance, permission, and choice to restore our minds back to sanity.

Recover Your Life

Happiness is not connected to an event or a goal, but in being able to notice beauty in the people and situations around you. It's a desire to show up and pay attention to life with an open heart. It's a personal choice to notice the ebb and flow of your successes and your failures without holding on to either. Happiness is a by-product of rest. It is not an end in itself, but a way to experience life. Through creative rest, social rest, and spiritual rest, you recover your ability to grow in fearless love, kindness, wisdom, and compassion. Your life becomes richer, your words more powerful, and your actions more purposeful. As you retreat from the business of busyness, you create space for the gifts of faith, choice, art, and productivity. In resting well, you recover your life.

What next steps do you need to take to find the rest you desire? Decide today to decree, "I choose my best life." Then join me for the next thirty days in the Sacred Rest Challenge. I pray our time together leads you into a lifelong recovery, renewal, and restoration experience in which your soul rejoices in the wide-open space of sacred rest (see Ps. 18:19).

Personal Rest Deficit Assessment Tool

This brief assessment tool is designed to help you quickly see which types of rest you are prone to be deficient in. For a more in-depth assessment, please visit RestQuiz.com, where you will find my comprehensive rest profile quiz. Upon completion of the online quiz, you will receive your personalized rest recommendations.

Place a check beside each statement that reflects how you feel:

Physical Rest

✓ You lack the energy needed to do all of the physical tasks on your to-do list.

___ You feel tired but have difficulty falling asleep.

___ You have a weak immune system with frequent colds and illnesses.

✓ You experience frequent muscle pain and soreness.

✓ You depend on substances to give you more energy (caffeine, energy bars, sugar).

___ You depend on substances to give you more rest (alcohol, pills, comfort foods).

Mental Rest

✓ You feel as if you can't keep up mentally with your to-do list.

✓ You experience irritation or frustration when thinking about your day.

___ You avoid some activities because you fear you will make an error or mess it up.

✓ You feel drowsy or as if you are in a mental fog during the day.

___ You snap at your family and coworkers about insignificant things.

___ You spend most of your day on tasks you find overwhelming.

Emotional Rest

✓ You have a tendency to focus on your failures and flaws.

___ You experience self-doubt and insecurity, which prevent you from trying new things.

✓ You constantly compensate for who you are with apologies or clarifications.

✓ You beat yourself up when you make even the slightest mistake.

___ You feel depressed or angry when you think about your life.

___ You exhibit excessive worrying or display feelings of anxiety about situations.

Spiritual Rest

✓ You feel decreased satisfaction and sense of accomplishment.

___ You feel helpless, hopeless, trapped, or defeated.

___ You feel like life is a total waste of energy and have no motivation.

√ You feel distant from God.

___ You experience suicidal thoughts and depression.

√ You feel numb and apathetic.

Social Rest

___ You feel alone in the world.

___ You feel detached from family and friends.

___ You are attracted to people who mistreat you or are abusive toward you.

___ You find it hard to maintain close relationships or make friends.

√ You isolate yourself from others.

___ You prefer online relationships over face-to-face relationships.

Sensory Rest

√ You have a sensitivity or an adverse reaction to loud sounds.

√ You experience blurry vision and/or eye pressure, fatigue, or strain.

___ You believe natural foods don't have any flavor and crave processed foods.

___ You dislike being hugged or touched by others.

___ You are desensitized to aromas others seem to smell easily.

√ You are unable to enjoy periodic sensory-rich experiences like concerts or fireworks.

Creative Rest

___ You always focus on the needs of others and don't consider your needs a priority.

___ You talk yourself out of self-care as if you don't deserve being cared for.

___ You feel you are being selfish whenever you consider doing something for yourself.

___ You do self-destructive things or make choices that sabotage your happiness.

___ You rarely feel your work is of value or that others appreciate your contributions.

___ You find it difficult to enjoy things in nature or in their natural state.

Look over each section. Three or more checks in a section suggest you are already suffering from a lack of rest in that area. One to two checks in a section suggest you are at an increased risk for burnout in that area. Now that you know which types of rest you've been missing, let's begin the journey into your well-rested life.

Thirty-Day Sacred Rest Challenge

Hey, fellow rest seeker! You finished the book, but your journey into sacred rest is just beginning. I'd love to walk this path with you for the next thirty days and give you some additional tips, tricks, and tactics for finding the rest you need. Head over to IChooseMyBestLife.com to sign up for the Sacred Rest Challenge. Each day I will send you a little encouragement to help you remember to return to rest in the middle of the busyness of life.

You are not in this alone. There is a whole community of rest seekers who want to celebrate your sacred rest moments with you. Join us by using #SacredRest when you post on Instagram, Facebook, Twitter, or Pinterest. Share the hidden beauty and captivating moments you discover as you experience the gifts of rest. Together let's lean into life and recline in the holy.

Acknowledgments

This book is the result of the thousands of stories shared with me by patients who want more energy and more opportunities to enjoy health, happiness, and the good things of life. To every woman who's shared from her vulnerability and strength—thank you. To every man who has openly shared his heart and struggles—thank you.

Les Stobbe, your encouragement and prayers are more than I could ask for in a literary agent. I am deeply thankful for your Christlike love for authors and for how you have mentored me over the years.

Long before I ever dreamed of publication, I held a copy of Joyce Meyer's *Battlefield of the Mind* in my hands and for the first time looked to see who published it. Not in a million years would I have thought at that time that I would one day hold a book with my name in the byline by the same publisher. Keren Baltzer and the FaithWords team, thank you for believing in me as an author and for your infectious excitement for this project.

Heidi and Sheryl, only God could have knitted our lives together in such an unbelievable way. Thank you both for our monthly prayer times and for your commitment to staying connected despite living thousands of miles apart.

Bobby, Tristan, and Isaiah, you guys are my heart and are the three greatest gifts God has given me. Thank you for believing in these words and for reminding me to rest in the midst of this writing journey. May every day God gives us together be rooted in reminders of His faithfulness, grace, and love.

Notes

Chapter 2: The Secret Life of the Well Rested

1. Pagels, Douglas. *These Are the Gifts I'd Like to Give to You: A Sourcebook of Joy and Encouragement.* Boulder, CO: Blue Mountain Arts, 1999 reprint.

Chapter 4: Physical Rest—When You Lay Your Body Down

1. National Sleep Foundation. "Annual Sleep in America Poll Exploring Connections with Communications, Technology Use, and Sleep." March 7, 2011. Web.
2. Jones, Caroline. "Why Am I Always Tired?" MSN.com Lifestyle. September 9, 2016. Web.
3. Fahmy, Sam. "Low-Intensity Exercise Reduces Fatigue Symptoms by 65 Percent, Study Finds." *UGA Today.* February 28, 2008. Web.

Chapter 5: Mental Rest—Quiet Cerebral Background Noise

1. Tanaka, Masaaki, Akira Ishii, and Yasuyoshi Watanabe. "Effects of Mental Fatigue on Brain Activity and Cognitive Performance: A Magnetoencephalography Study." *Anatomy & Physiology.* S4:002 (2015). doi:10.4172/2161-0940.
2. Mitchell, Rae Lynn. "The Body and the Brain: Impact of Mental, Physical Exertion on Fatigue Development." *ScienceDaily.* July 30, 2015. Web.

Chapter 6: Emotional Rest—Acknowledge Your Current Truth

1. "Genesis 3: The Fall." The Holy Bible: New International Version. Grand Rapids, MI: Zondervan, 2005.

2. Hatfield, Elaine, John T. Cacioppo, and Richard L. Rapson. *Emotional Contagion*. Cambridge: Cambridge University Press, 1994.

3. Motluk, Alison. "How the Brain Detects the Emotions of Others." *New Scientist*. Daily News. May 12, 2008. Web.

4. Carter, Sherrie Bourg. "Emotions Are Contagious—Choose Your Company Wisely." *Psychology Today*. High-Octane Women. October 12, 2012. Web.

Chapter 7: Spiritual Rest—Enter Your Personal Sanctuary

1. Plato and Robin Waterfield. *Meno and Other Dialogues*. Oxford: Oxford University Press, 2005.

2. "Broken." Merriam-Webster.com. Accessed February 2, 2017. Web.

3. Hodges, Glenda F. *When Spirituality and Medicine Disconnect: Gaining the World and Losing God's Promise*. Bloomington, IN: AuthorHouse, 2014.

4. "Your Brain on Prayer." *Discovery Science*. Through the Wormhole. August 3, 2012. Web.

5. Davis, Jeanie Lerche. "Can Prayer Heal?" WebMD. Accessed February 2, 2017. Web.

6. "Mark 8:29." The Holy Bible: New International Version. Grand Rapids, MI: Zondervan, 2005.

Chapter 8: Social Rest—Find Solace in Another

1. "The Health Benefits of Strong Relationships." *Harvard Women's Health Watch*. Harvard Health Publications. December 2010. Web.

2. "Friendships: Enrich Your Life and Improve Your Health." Mayo Clinic. Adult Health. September 28, 2016. Web.

Chapter 9: Sensory Rest—Remove External Distractions

1. Smith, Sandy. "Most Americans Experience Digital Eye Strain from Overexposure to Computers." *EHS Today*. July 6, 2016. Web.

2. "Noise and Hearing Loss Prevention." Centers for Disease Control and Prevention. October 19, 2016. Web.

Chapter 10: Creative Rest—Soak in Beauty and Light

1. "Genesis 1:1–2:3: The Beginning." The Holy Bible: New International Version. Grand Rapids, MI: Zondervan, 2005.

2. Elwell, Walter A., ed. *Baker Encyclopedia of the Bible*, vol. 2, p. 1840. Grand Rapids, MI: Baker Book House, 1988.

3. "Exodus 33:14." The Holy Bible: New International Version. Grand Rapids, MI: Zondervan, 2005.

4. "Vitamin D and Health." *The Nutrition Source*. Harvard School of Public Health, May 26, 2015. Web.

5. Stewart, Lorna. "Oh, Why Do We Like to Be Beside the Seaside?" BBC News. September 28, 2013. Web.

6. Schwartz, Tony. "The 90-Minute Solution: How Building in Periods of Renewal Can Change Your Work and Your Life." *The Huffington Post*. May 18, 2010. Web.

7. Pozin, Ilya. "Your Body's Circadian Rhythm Can Be Your Productivity Secret." *The Next Web*. February 25, 2014. Web.

Chapter 11: Give It a Rest

1. "Hosea 4:6." The Holy Bible: New International Version. Grand Rapids, MI: Zondervan, 2005.

Chapter 14: The Gift of Reflection

1. "Reflection." Merriam-Webster.com. Accessed February 2, 2017. Web.

2. "Deuteronomy 31:6." The Holy Bible: New International Version. Grand Rapids, MI: Zondervan, 2005.

3. "Ephesians 3:20." The ESV Study Bible (English Standard Version). Wheaton, IL: Crossway, 1970.

4. Tate, Karl. "'Blood Moons' Explained: What Causes a Lunar Eclipse Tetrad?" Space.com. September 18, 2015. Web.

5. "Learning By Thinking: How Reflection Improves Performance." hbswk.hbs.edu. Accessed February 2, 2017. Web.

6. Heen, Erik M. and Philip D. W. Krey, eds. " 'Rest' Is Not Running to the Old," in *New Testament X: Hebrews.* Ancient Christian Commentary on Scripture, p. 61. Downers Grove, IL: InterVarsity Press, 2005.

Chapter 15: The Gift of Freedom

1. "John 10:10." The Holy Bible: New International Version. Grand Rapids, MI: Zondervan, 2005.
2. "Exodus 12:7–13." The Holy Bible: New International Version. Grand Rapids, MI: Zondervan, 2005.
3. "Exodus 3:13–14." The Holy Bible: New International Version. Grand Rapids, MI: Zondervan, 2005.

Chapter 16: The Gift of Acceptance

1. "Matthew 3:17." The Holy Bible: English Standard Version. Wheaton, IL: Crossway Bibles, 2001.

Chapter 17: The Gift of Exchange

1. Spurgeon, C. H. "The Christ-Given Rest," in *The Metropolitan Tabernacle Pulpit Sermons*, vol. 39, p. 114. London: Passmore & Alabaster, 1893.
2. Knowles, Andrew. *The Bible Guide*, 1st Augsburg books ed., p. 421. Minneapolis, MN: Augsburg, 2001.
3. Green, Michael. *The Message of Matthew: The Kingdom of Heaven*, p. 143. Leicester, England; Downers Grove, IL: InterVarsity Press, 2001.

Chapter 19: The Gift of Cessation

1. "Judaism 101: Shabbat." JewFAQ.org. Accessed February 3, 2017. Web.

Chapter 20: The Gift of Art

1. "Art." *English Oxford Living Dictionaries*. Accessed February 3, 2017. Web.
2. "Andre Gide Quotes." ThinkExist.com. Accessed February 3, 2017. Web.

Chapter 21: The Gift of Communication

1. "World's Weirdest: Honey Bee Dance Moves." *National Geographic*. 2014. Web.

2. "William Glasser Quotes." ThinkExist.com. Accessed February 3, 2017. Web.

3. Jobe, Kari. "The More I Seek You." Recorded July 11, 2006. Gateway Worship. CD.

Chapter 22: The Gift of Productivity

1. "Quotes by Mary O'Connor." QuotationsBook.com. Accessed February 3, 2017. Web.

2. "Abide." Merriam-Webster.com. Accessed January 30, 2017. Web.

3. "Matthew 19:26." *The Holy Bible: New International Version*. Grand Rapids, MI: Zondervan, 2005.

4. Elwell, Walter A., ed. *Evangelical Commentary on the Bible*, vol. 3, John 15:1. Grand Rapids, MI: Baker Book House, 1995.

5. Huffington, Arianna. *Thrive: The Third Metric to Redefining Success and Creating a Life of Well-Being, Wisdom, and Wonder*. New York: Harmony, 2014.

Chapter 23: The Gift of Choice

1. Dalton-Smith, Saundra. *Set Free to Live Free: Breaking Through the 7 Lies Women Tell Themselves*. Grand Rapids, MI: Revell, 2011.

Chapter 24: The Gift of Faith

1. Hurnard, Hannah. *Hinds' Feet on High Places*. Blacksburg, VA: Wilder Publications, 2010.

2. Dalton-Smith, Saundra. *Come Empty: Pour Out Life's Hurts and Receive God's Healing Love*. Raleigh, NC: Lighthouse of the Carolinas, SonRise Devotionals, 2015.

Chapter 25: I Choose My Best Life

1. Healthways. "Gallup-Healthways Well-Being Index." Accessed February 3, 2017. Web.

About the Author

Dr. Saundra Dalton-Smith is a board-certified internal medicine physician, author, and speaker. She shares with audiences nationwide on the topics of eliminating limiting emotions and overcoming destructive mind-sets so you can live fully, love boldly, and rest intentionally. Dr. Dalton-Smith is a national and international media resource on the mind-body-spirit connection and has been featured in many publications including *Woman's Day*, *Redbook*, and *First for Women* magazine. She has written two award-winning books, *Set Free to Live Free: Breaking Through the 7 Lies Women Tell Themselves* and *Come Empty: Pour Out Life's Hurts and Receive God's Healing Love*. She is one of the 100 experts included in the 2017 book *Good Housekeeping Doctors' Secrets: Fight Disease, Relieve Pain, and Live a Healthy Life with Practical Advice from 100 Top Medical Experts*. She blogs at IChooseMyBestLife.com, where she shares tips to help you heal from the inside out, and she has an active medical practice in Alabama, where she lives with her husband and two boys.

If you would like to invite Dr. Saundra to speak at your next event, you can contact her at DrDaltonSmith@IChooseMyBestLife.com.

www.facebook.com/DrSaundraDaltonSmith

twitter.com/DrDaltonSmith